AGAINST ALL ODDS

YOUNG READERS' EDITION

CRAIG CHALLEN AND RICHARD HARRIS

WITH ELLIS HENICAN

EDITED BY NAN McNAB

PENGUIN BOOKS

PENGUIN BOOKS

UK | USA | Canada | Ireland | Australia
India | New Zealand | South Africa | China

Penguin Random House Australia is part of the Penguin Random House group of companies whose addresses can be found at global.penguinrandomhouse.com.

First published by Viking, an imprint of Penguin Random House Australia Pty Ltd, in 2019

This young readers' edition published by Penguin Books, an imprint of Penguin Random House Australia Pty Ltd, in 2022

Cover images by Shutterstock, JITTRAPON KAICOME/AFP via Getty Images and Heather Endall (back cover)
Map on p. 256 reproduced by permission of Association Pyreneenne de Speleologie/ Unsworth/Harper/Ellis May 2019
Design by Tony Palmer © Penguin Random House Australia Pty Ltd
Typeset in 11.5/15.5pt Minion Pro and 10.5/15.5pt DIN by Midland Typesetters, Australia

Printed and bound in Australia by Griffin Press, an accredited ISO AS/NZS 14001 Environmental Management Systems printer

A catalogue record for this book is available from the National Library of Australia

ISBN 978 0 14 377820 2 (Paperback)

Penguin Random House Australia uses papers that are natural and recyclable products, made from wood grown in sustainable forests. The logging and manufacture processes are expected to conform to the environmental regulations of the country of origin.

penguin.com.au

We at Penguin Random House Australia acknowledge that Aboriginal and Torres Strait Islander peoples are the Traditional Custodians and the first storytellers of the lands on which we live and work. We honour Aboriginal and Torres Strait Islander peoples' continuous connection to Country, waters, skies and communities. We celebrate Aboriginal and Torres Strait Islander stories, traditions and living cultures; and we pay our respects to Elders past and present.

AGAINST ALL ODDS

YOUNG READERS' EDITION

In June 2018, for seventeen days, the world watched and held its breath as the Wild Boars soccer team were trapped deep in a cave in Thailand. Marooned beyond flooded cave passages after unexpected rains, they were finally rescued, one-by-one, against almost impossible odds, by an international cave-diving team that included Australians Dr Richard 'Harry' Harris and Dr Craig Challen.

Harry and Craig were chosen for their medical expertise and cave diving knowledge, but this dangerous rescue asked so much more of them. They had to remain calm under extreme pressure and intense scrutiny, adapt to constantly changing circumstances and, most importantly, build trust among the rescue team and with the young boys and their coach, whose lives were in their hands.

Against All Odds **is the astonishing and moving story of courage, determination and compassion told by two Aussie heroes, who were made joint Australians of the Year for their crucial role in the rescue. The story of the rescue is also now portrayed in a major motion picture, Netflix series and National Geographic documentary.**

To my mother, who taught me what is important in life. And to Heather, who has put up with a lot.

Craig Challen

For my father, Jim. He took a small boy out in a boat and ignited a passion for the underwater world that will last a lifetime.

Richard Harris

FOREWORD

The world was riveted by the news coming out of Thailand. Twelve local boys and their soccer coach trapped by early rains deep inside a cave system, cut off from the outside world, imprisoned in absolute darkness, with little hope of rescue. As rescue efforts escalated, ultimately bringing in thousands of rescue experts, divers, military and throngs of media, the situation only seemed bleaker by the day. The boys were found alive by two British cave divers who pushed through strong currents and zero visibility over four kilometres into the bowels of the mountain, but the rains were coming soon, which would wipe out all hope of extracting the stranded soccer team.

Into that nightmare in slow motion stepped Australian cave divers Richard 'Harry' Harris and Craig Challen.

They had advanced cave-diving skills and they were doctors, which made them the most important members of the proposed rescue mission. It soon became clear that the boys would have to be sedated and brought out of the cave unconscious, for both their own protection against deadly panic, and for the protection of the rescue divers.

Cave divers may differ in background and personality, but they all share the same rare combination of intelligence and grit. They survive the seeming impossible through an absolute focus on the task. They pit their wit and their stamina against the most fearsome physical environment imaginable. They understand the extreme risk they take diving under thousands of feet of rock, where the only way out is back the way you came in, and where you cannot simply swim to the surface if something goes wrong with you or your gear.

They reduce that risk as much as possible through intelligence, training and meticulous planning. But they can never reduce the risk to zero. They accept the risk that remains, what I call the X-factor, because they are driven by the true explorer spirit.

Cave divers are some of the most self-reliant people on the planet. Even if you dive as a team, like Craig and Harry do, you're still alone on the dive. When squeezing through passages so narrow you can't wear your air cylinder on your back, with the rock pressing down on your spine and up on your belly, in water so murky you can't see your hand in front of your dive mask, miles in from the entrance, beyond all possible hope of rescue – you're on your own. The other guy might only be a few feet away, but he or she can't help you.

Cave diving is both highly technical and also the most primal human-mind-against-nature challenge that I can imagine.

When I was reading Harry and Craig's story, I was biting my nails during some of the sections where they take us through the rescue dives, moment by moment. Every decision they made was literally life or death, for those trapped kids, and possibly for themselves.

I was particularly struck by the soul-torturing ethical dilemmas each man faced as a medical professional. No one had ever drugged a child into unconsciousness, put diving gear on them, and then dragged them out through miles of flooded tunnels, including constrictions so small a single diver could barely slither through, blinded by silt, doing it all by feel. It's one thing to make decisions for yourself, as an explorer and adventurer, quite another to make them for a trusting and innocent child.

There was no precedent to what they were doing, and no guidelines for how it might even be accomplished. They were making it up as they went along, with the eyes of the world upon them. Not only the eyes of a fickle media, but also the eyes of the Thai authorities and the terrified parents. Imagine that dread weight upon their shoulders, as each decision was taken: what drugs to use? what dosages? and how to maintain that level of sedation? Each boy would need additional injections throughout the hours of their rescue. The rescue divers might even have to inject these kids through their wetsuits in some dark, flooded passage. They didn't know if they'd be bringing out live boys by the end of the dive. And if the first died, or the second, would you go on and inject that third kid and try it again? So many unknowns, so many variables. It must have seemed like madness, but at the same time their relentless logic said it was the only answer.

In reading this book you'll live it, hour by hour, minute by minute, as it was experienced by two divers at the front line of the rescue. Harry and Craig repeatedly stress how many skilled and heroic divers were involved in the rescue besides themselves – the British cavers who found the boys and helped with the extraction, the Thai Navy SEALs who stayed with them in their subterranean prison and kept them healthy and hopeful, and many others.

Before it was finished, the rescue effort involved more than 10,000 people, including over 100 divers, 900 police officers and 2000 soldiers. A hundred government agencies from all over the world participated. But in the end it boiled down to a handful of skilled divers who swam those boys out. This book puts you there, deep inside that flooded cave, experiencing it firsthand.

It is an inspirational story of what we humans are capable of when we come together to help others. It chronicles the international outpouring of empathy and effort to save those innocent lost boys. It is also an epic underwater adventure, the stuff of novels and movies, told in a humble, matter-of-fact way. But this isn't some Hollywood screenplay – this actually happened.

James Cameron

CONTENTS

INTRODUCTION TO THIS EDITION

Life can lead you to the most unexpected places. In this book, you will read about the extraordinary rescue that Harry and I participated in over a number of tumultuous days in July 2018.

In hindsight, we were as prepared as anyone could be for such an unusual event. But we would never in our wildest dreams have imagined it. We're not professional rescuers, we're just a couple of ordinary people who cave dive, an unusual hobby most people had never heard of prior to the Tham Luang rescue.

Our readiness for the rescue came from a life of adventuring and exploration, and this is a life that I would recommend. Many readers will say to themselves, 'I could never do something like cave diving'. But this is the worst thing you can do, putting limits on yourself before you have even tried for no reason other than fear of the unknown. Cave diving and other adventures have built qualities in us – strength, resilience and mental toughness – that have made us the people we are today and led us to places we could not have imagined.

Aside from the rescue, one of the achievements I am most proud of, as well, is developing expertise in deep-cave-diving exploration. This kind of cave diving happens in water deeper that 200 metres. There are perhaps a dozen people throughout the world that have done dives such as this, and when Harry and I started we did not think we could ever be part of that group. There is certainly nothing special about my physical or mental abilities or courage. But slowly I built knowledge and expertise, until one day I realised that the limits I had previously believed in were not really there at all. I was able to do so much more and go so much further than I knew.

There is no doubt that accidents can sometimes happen in adventure sports like cave diving. But cave divers are not adrenaline junkies with a death wish. We love life as much as, if not more than, anyone else. The difference is that we enjoy challenging and extending ourselves, testing our mettle to find our limits, control risk and defeat fear. And every challenge pursued, whether successful or not, builds our capability and strength as adventurers.

Of course, not everyone is going to become a cave diver, or participate in extreme sports. But we all participate in the great adventure of life. At the risk of sounding clichéd, you only get one shot at this life, so make it a good one. Whatever you choose to pursue, do it to the best of your ability, uninhibited by imagined limits that you place upon yourself.

I hope you enjoy our story, but I also hope that you get more from it than just a great tale. I hope you learn how challenges prepare us for the trials and unexpected obstacles that pop up in our journey through life.

The life of an adventurer is not for everyone. But everyone can be adventurous in their life and we urge them to do so. You never know where it will take you.

Craig Challen

After the rescue of the young boys from the cave in Thailand, we were filled with admiration for how courageous the lads had been. They spent 10 very long days sitting in the dark at the back of that cave, without any hope or expectation of rescue. I wondered how I might have fared under similar circumstances? Would I have found the courage that these boys demonstrated? I believe that most of us are not inherently brave, but rather it is something we have to work on. We do this by challenging ourselves throughout life by doing things outside our comfort zone. In other words, courage can be learned.

After the cave rescue was over, a correspondent from the USA described me as a 'unicorn' because of the rare and improbable combination of skills I brought to the rescue. Experience in cave diving, an interest in rescuing people from flooded caves and my work as an anaesthetist. In fact, he was not quite right, as I personally know several other anaesthetists with similar skills. But it did make me think. As a young man I grew up lacking confidence and struggled to find something I was good at. Team sports failed to excite me and I definitely didn't shine on the field. I was disengaged at school, only just managing to get my head down at the last minute to achieve sufficient grades to go to university. But I was lucky that I had found a passion in life at a very early age – exploring the ocean.

After the cave rescue, Craig and I became Joint Australians of the Year for 2019. In the process, we gave many talks around the country including to school students. And I came to realise that every one of us is a unicorn. Every one of us has a unique combination of skills and characteristics, and hopefully there is a custom-made place in life for all of us. That's not to say that everyone will end up being involved in a Thai cave rescue! But we should all take advantage of every opportunity that comes our way, for one never knows where such moments will lead.

We all struggle to find courage and our place in life. Courage and confidence come in many forms and can build over time. We all have unique skills – sometimes we just need time to discover what they are.

'THEY'RE ALL GOING TO DIE'

HARRY

It was the mission we'd all been training for, a life-or-death rescue in remote northern Thailand, deep inside a flooded mountain cave. The whole world was watching. The chances were disturbingly slim. Anyone who knew anything about cave rescue knew that. Thirteen young people were huddled in the chilly darkness, one monsoonal downpour away from the end of their lives.

And where was I?

I was 7022 kilometres away, at my usual post in the operating theatre of Flinders Private Hospital in Adelaide, making sure a patient didn't wake up from her anaesthesia. I love being in theatre. But *man*! I'd never felt so far from the action in my life.

Early that morning before work, a message had popped up on my phone. It was from the legendary British cave diver Rick Stanton, who had raced to the scene with fellow Brit John Volanthen to help save the stranded members of the Wild Boars soccer team.

'Could you sedate someone and dive them out?' he wanted to know.

Rick must be desperate, I thought. Otherwise, he'd never ask a question so absurd. As an anaesthetist and a diver, I thought the very idea sounded preposterous. You'd kill the kid for sure.

'Sedation not an option,' I replied. I could think of a hundred ways it could end in tragedy and not a single way it might succeed.

It was Wednesday, 4 July 2018. The boys had been trapped in Tham Luang cave since the evening of Saturday, 23 June – well over a week – and the outlook was grim. Rick hated what he found at the cave: a circus of ill-trained thrill-seekers, gung-ho military types, overwhelmed government officials and gullible journalists from around the world sending out ridiculously optimistic updates about the chances of saving the boys. Things were so chaotic at the cave, Rick confided, that he was ready to pack up his dive gear and fly home.

Thankfully, Rick and his guys decided to stay. They clipped on their tanks, spat in their face masks and pressed on. They would, of course, be the first divers to locate the twelve frightened soccer players and their 25-year-old assistant coach, shivering on top of a muddy hill more than two and a half kilometres in. But locating the team was one thing. Navigating the cave's narrow passages and sharp, jutting rocks in zero visibility to guide the boys out – that was something else entirely. That, I hoped, was where Craig Challen, my long-time dive buddy, and I might still fit in.

Ever since we'd seen the first stories about the boys lost

in the cave, Craig and I had been angling to help. Both of us had trained for years in underground rescue. Both of us had decades of medical experience, too – I was an anaesthetist and critical-care doctor, and Craig was a veterinary surgeon. We'd played key roles in a couple of harrowing body-recovery operations. But so far, we had never been part of a live rescue involving so many people, or in such treacherous conditions as this. But no one had asked us to come to Thailand – *yet*.

Every man and his dog had a theory about how to get these poor children out of the cave. Drill through the limestone from above. Pump the water out from below. Give the boys a crash course in scuba diving and swim them out. Not one of them showed any promise. The billionaire tech promoter Elon Musk would soon be promoting his own creative schemes, which included an inflatable tunnel and a minisub. Or how about leaving the boys in the cave for five or six months, with food, clean water, space blankets and maybe some video games – and then walking them out after the rainy season? Everybody was utterly perplexed.

'I should be over there helping,' I texted Rick. 'Craig and I are happy to provide any assistance.'

A couple of hours later, he texted again, explaining exactly what we'd soon be facing. 'You're going to dive to the end of the cave,' he warned. 'You're going to see these kids. They're all looking healthy and happy and smiley. Then you're going to swim away and probably leave them all to die. Be mindful of that before you say yes with too much enthusiasm.'

It was only after arriving in Thailand that Craig and I understood Rick's warning. The plight of the boys was far more dire than any outsider realised.

Against All Odds is the true inside story of the greatest cave rescue ever, much of it revealed here for the very first time. The heartbreak and the triumph. The far-fetched strategies that were laughed out of Thailand and the one that would ultimately save the day. Most of all, it's the story of the remarkable band of characters from around the world who were determined to save these stranded boys no matter what the risk.

- Rick and his mates, world-class divers who looked like a ragtag collection of middle-aged hobbyists;
- three Thai Navy SEALs – the greatest babysitters ever;
- a charismatic Thai military doctor who would keep the children healthy, both mentally and physically, long enough to be saved;
- the team's assistant coach, who would guide the boys through their ordeal with incredible devotion and a deep, spiritual calm;
- Craig and me.

Craig and I weren't certain what we could do that might help save the lives of those boys, but we would soon find out.

I

HOPING

1

WHO'S HARRY?

HARRY

First, the name. Officially, it's Richard James Dunbar Harris, though pretty much everyone calls me Harry, except for my father – for some reason he liked to call me Bert.

My thirst for life and taste for adventure came from my family, my dad especially.

My family

From the time I was a little tacker, I loved being outdoors. My parents took us on camping weekends and fishing in small boats. We knew people with beach houses and spent every summer by the sea. I loved swimming and snorkelling and trying to catch fish in the ocean. The outdoor life was for me.

Dad was a huge influence. He was an affable, lovable, large-bellied bloke who grew up on South Australia's Murray River and enjoyed the good life. His father and his father's brother had both died young from heart disease.

'I don't know if you should marry me,' my father told my mother. 'I'll probably just die like my father and uncle did.' But he always said, 'If I'm only here for a short time, I might as well make it a good time!'

Though he was a respected surgeon, he had friends from every imaginable walk of life. Funny characters were always dropping by: tradesmen, academics, outdoorsmen, some mate who was tinkering with a boat motor in our shed. Everyone had a story, my father taught me.

Dad especially loved spending time with his birds. We had three backyard aviaries filled with parrots and other exotic species. I became his main bird wrangler. 'Bert,' he'd say, 'go in and grab that green eclectus parrot over there.' That's a big brute from northern Australia and New Guinea with a very powerful beak.

'The eclectus?' I'd say, reluctant. 'They're a bit nippy, aren't they?'

'Just grab it, Bert,' my father would insist. 'It needs worming.'

I'd fetch the net and toss it over the bird. Then I'd hold it so my father could inject the medicine into its belly, giving the bird every opportunity to chomp down on my thumb.

'*AAAAAAAARGH! Dad, it's got me! Hurry up!*'

'Be gentle with it!' he'd snap.

'*Are you kidding? It just about took my thumb off!*'

He and my mother often had to yank me back from some crazy idea, like digging up the rose garden and replacing it with a terrarium for my pet reptiles.

Mum was just as loving as Dad, but she could be a bit stroppy. She ruled the house. Maid Marion, we called her, or

Winnie the Wettex, a nod to her beloved sponge cloth. She was constantly picking up after us and supplying us with food. If you wandered into the kitchen to help, she would shoo you out. Which left me domestically challenged and a little bit lazy.

Growing up

I was an average student – bright, but cheeky and disruptive. I laughed whenever I got into trouble, which didn't help. My best friend in school was Sam Hall. I became the extra son in the Hall family. I'd gobble up Mrs Hall's famous roast lamb and gravy, then tell Mum, 'Your gravy's not like Mrs Hall's.'

Sam and I shared our first experience of true outdoor discomfort: a school hiking trip through the Adelaide Hills in winter. We were absolutely miserable. It was raining and cold, no one could start a fire, there was no proper food to eat, the tent leaked and the sleeping-bags got wet.

'This is rubbish,' I moaned to Sam. But then we decided we'd turn the whole thing into a joke. When we got lost, it was 'character-building'. When the sleeping-bags were drenched, that was 'character-building'. It changed everything.

I remember thinking, *How you react to something makes a difference*. It determines whether you'll to enjoy it or not, or whether you'll cope.

Pat Harbison was a renowned marine biologist and one of my father's friends. When I was about thirteen, I'd been out spearfishing in South Australia's Coffin Bay. I had speared half-a-dozen pretty reef fish.

'Show me what you've got,' Pat said as I laid the fish out on the beach. 'What's this one called?' she asked.

'I don't really know,' I admitted.

'That's a zebra fish,' she said. She described what it ate and where it lived. 'You can't really eat it, of course,' she added.

'Okay,' I said.

She went through the fish one by one, teaching me about them and adding each time: 'Of course, you can't eat that one, either.'

Finally, a light-bulb moment: I'd just murdered six fascinating and beautiful fish for no reason at all. I was really embarrassed. Without any prodding or preaching, my father's friend had made me think, *In the future, why don't I just spear the ones we can eat?* From that day forward, I wanted to be a marine biologist.

I took an open-water diving course when I was fifteen and loved being underwater and seeing giant cuttlefish, blue-ringed octopus and red snapper. I learned about all the equipment, and the fact that it seemed a little dangerous was exciting. On a warm, sunny February afternoon, Sam and I were in the Gulf St Vincent with Ron Allum, our diving instructor, and two young women. We were heading back to the dock around 5 p.m. after exploring a shipwreck when the waves in the gulf really began to kick up. We went down one wave into the back of the next, flipping our small dive boat end over end and dumping all five of us into the water.

The boat was swamped, and the engine wouldn't start. We were much too far out to swim to shore, but we were all wearing wetsuits and quickly donned life jackets. All we could do was cling to the boat and wait. As darkness fell and the lights of Adelaide twinkled in the distance, the sea got rougher and the temperature dropped.

Around three in the morning, the floorboards of the boat began to pop out and chunks of the buoyancy foam floated away. Even I was thinking, *This really might be it.*

At daybreak, we could tell we'd drifted with the tide. Down to the south, we could see boats and aeroplanes searching. At last an old timber boat chugged towards us. An old fisherman called out: 'Are you the blokes that are lost? Yeah, I thought you'd be about here.'

He'd studied the tides and the winds and pinpointed us exactly. We climbed onto his boat, where he served us coffee and Vegemite sandwiches, then towed our waterlogged dive boat back to the ramp like a submarine.

I've always been proud of the fact that I went back to boating and diving after that harrowing night on the water. I decided the rewards outweighed the risks. Sam and I learned from the experience. We both became safer boaters, making sure we were always equipped with flares and a radio, and that the anchor rope was tied to the boat. I still had a lot of growing up to do, but my dad would still let me take his little boat and his camping gear and head out for another week of adventure with my friends, getting away from our parents' supervision and testing ourselves.

When it came time to apply to university in 1981, I was still keen to study marine biology. Then one of my cousins, who was in his second year of marine biology up in Queensland, said, 'Don't do it, there's no work.' So I went for veterinary science instead, choosing medicine as my backup. On school holidays, I had worked as a jackeroo on a sheep station near Broken Hill. I really liked animals, but I didn't get into the veterinary program at Murdoch University in Perth, where Craig would study a couple of years later. Instead, I ended up at the new and progressive School of Medicine at Flinders University, which had a strong commitment to public health around the world.

The campus was nothing like my posh private boys school. For the first time ever, I could see what a sheltered, narrow upbringing I'd had. It was a bit of a wake-up call for me, a time to broaden my horizons. It took me a few years, but I got over myself eventually.

I made friends. I had fun. A bit too much perhaps! After failing and repeating the first year I settled down and never failed another exam. I was starting to grow up.

Of the many different fields of medicine, I liked anaesthesia best. The fact that you really did hold the patient's life in your hands. But I also enjoyed travelling overseas and training in rural areas where you were expected to do everything. Treat diseases. Perform surgery. Deal with public-health crises. You really could save people's lives.

I joined the university dive club, became one of the dive instructors and was eventually elected president. One day in 1985, a few of us headed down to Mount Gambier in the south-eastern corner of the state and signed up for a cave-diving course.

I can't pretend I loved it. It was wintertime, rainy and cold, and I was dressed in an old wetsuit. The water was around 15 degrees Celsius, and the cave was a grimy hole, full of weeds. The training was robust, and the course emphasised safety. But we were in a very unpleasant environment, and I couldn't help but wonder: *Why does anyone do this?*

When I got home, I joined the Cave Divers Association of Australia, but I thought: *Cave diving is nothing I'll carry on with, that's for sure.*

A year or so later, I began spending a lot of time with a smart, pretty young med student named Fiona Allen. We'd known each other as friends and colleagues for two or three years before I started looking at her in a very different way. 'Cave diving?' she said to me. 'That's dangerous, isn't it?' I was happy to drop it entirely if she was worried about it.

Adult life

Fiona and I married in 1990, and my life headed off in other directions, especially when our first son, James, arrived in 1996, followed the next year by Charlie, son number two. As a young doctor in training, I was drawn to the edgier side of medicine, flying off to emergency cases in a specially equipped helicopter.

I finished my training as an anaesthetist at a small but busy district hospital in the northern New Zealand town of Whangarei. Part of that work involved flying into rugged environments without all the equipment and staff you'd find in a proper operating theatre – cardiac cases far from any hospital, vehicle accidents with multiple injuries, serious traumas at far-flung worksites. Life-or-death medicine! Those patients called on everything I had in me, producing a fierce rush of adrenaline. I always did my best, and I could usually make a difference.

'You're always dealing with people who are on the brink of death,' Fiona said to me one day. We worked in the same hospitals in those days. I was usually part of a resuscitation team, looking after heart-attack patients. 'I'm happy to see you at those cases,' she said. 'You always look so calm.'

If the person in charge is falling apart, a patient's chances can deteriorate rapidly. Someone has to at least *appear* in control.

In 2000, our daughter, Millie, was born. Things were busy around the Harris house. One of the techs operating the hyperbaric (or decompression) chamber at the Diving and Hyperbaric unit was a former police diver. One day he began to talk about the sinkhole where he'd trained. It sounded like a great dive. He offered to set things up with the landowner and he sounded so enthusiastic I thought: *Why not?*

I hadn't given much thought to cave diving in a while. But Sam Hall and I ended up driving to the farm, finding the sinkhole and jumping in. The water was freezing cold, but I had a wetsuit. I just went for a shallow, quick dive. And I was blown away.

The water was crystal clear with a slight tinge of blue. The sun was shining down through the mouth of the caves I went down about twenty metres. The cave fell away below me and I could see everything. As soon as I climbed out of that sparkling water, I said to Sam, 'What have I been missing? I didn't know it could be like this.'

I rejoined the Cave Divers Association. I managed to convince Fiona I wasn't going to kill myself and leave her a widow with three young children. I took the basic cave-diving course again. I was hooked. Soon, I was flying off to all the advanced courses I could find.

In 2004 Fiona and I left to spend two years living and working in Vanuatu, a former French colony in the Pacific Ocean that is now an independent island republic. What Vanuatu lacked in modern sophistication, it more than made up for with beautiful, fascinating, water-filled caves. And I was, it seemed, almost the only person in the whole country who had any interest in diving them. I couldn't believe my good fortune. I had my own set of virgin caves. No human being had ever set foot in most of them. That's where I caught the real exploration bug. That was it; I was obsessed.

2
MAKING CRAIG
CRAIG

Like Harry, I had a circuitous route to Tham Luang cave. At an early age, I came to appreciate the thrills of outdoor adventure, but other things kept pulling me away.

My family

My father, Bruce Challen, worked for a bank, living and working in one of many small towns for a couple of years. My mother, born Patricia Patton, came off a farm in Trundle, New South Wales. Her mother was especially keen on education for girls, which was unusual for the time.

Even so, there were only two career options open to my mother and aunt.

Teaching or nursing? Which will it be?

These were smart, independent young women. *Nursing*, both of them announced. After finishing her training and working for a few years, my mother took an even bolder leap. She headed 4500 kilometres out to rugged Western Australia and settled in the north-western town of Port Hedland, where women were scarce and most men were either miners or cattle farmers. When this bright young nurse moved into town and showed up at the local hospital, everyone was very happy to see her – but no one more than the young, single manager at the local bank.

My parents married in 1963. I arrived, kicking and screaming, in 1965, the first of my parents' four children – two boys and two girls. During my teens Dad bought a small farm in rural Gidgegannup, forty kilometres outside Perth, where we moved to raise sheep. We soon realised that the country was a fine place for kids to have adventures.

Growing up

That move to the country turned out to be the formative experience of my life. It's where I really took to outdoor adventure. I would leave the house first thing in the morning with my brother Ray, and not come home until dark, except maybe to check in for lunch. Our farm bordered a national park and the Avon River, so there were endless rocks to climb and cool places to explore. I just loved being outside. I still do. It makes me feel alive.

Good marks came easily in school, but, like Harry, I wasn't a sporty kid. I much preferred hiking, riding and hunting for trouble with Ray and my mates.

From my father, I learned the importance of hard work and dogged determination. From Mum, I learned the value of relentless inquiry, an openness to the opinions of others and a willingness to change.

In the country and the suburbs, we'd always had lots of animals, and I was comfortable around them. We considered our dogs part of the family. I loved riding horses and had spent a lot of time working with sheep and cattle. I had an aptitude for science, and I enjoyed working with my hands. Being a veterinarian seemed like the obvious choice.

I hit a bit of a rough patch near the end of high school, but somehow knuckled down in the last few weeks of my final year and did well enough in my exams to get into whatever university course I wanted. It was 1982. I was seventeen. I went with the vet option.

Everything about the vet school sounded cool! There was a fully fledged veterinary hospital, where students and academic clinical staff cared for all kinds of animals, from cats, dogs and birds to horses, cattle and even the occasional unlucky kangaroo. There were courses in wildlife, exotic pets and conservation medicine – and students helped to treat the lions, elephants and giraffes at the world-class Perth Zoo.

I had a great time in vet school. I could have studied harder but I did well enough, and along the way I discovered that what most appealed to me was surgery. I liked doing things with my hands, but I also discovered I had a surgeon's personality. The best surgeons are meticulous, intensely focused and sometimes downright obsessed, but they combine those qualities with a certain derring-do. Surgeons are the swashbucklers of medicine. I didn't want to sit in a consulting room all day, performing check-ups, giving vaccinations and calming nervous clients, whether animal or human. Surgery was where the action was, and where I wanted to be.

What vet school really taught me, though, was problem-solving and self-reliance. I gained skills that would serve me for the rest of my life.

Adult life

I started my career as a locum, filling in for other vets, which was excellent training. I was often dropped in at the deep end and had to think and learn quickly. After a detour into business, which went well enough, I returned to veterinary practice in 1990, working at Joondalup Veterinary Hospital.

By early 1993, my partner was Lianne Hulse. We decided to start our own veterinary practice. I did the clinical work, and she handled the management. By day I did clinical work. By night, in between after-hours calls from clients, I worked as builder, plasterer and painter to get the place in reasonable shape. But with hard work the practice thrived, and after a couple of years we started another a short distance away. Eventually we built up a network of clinics that would become Vetwest Animal Hospitals, the largest provider of veterinary services in Western Australia.

But by the time I reached my late thirties, I was starting to ask myself, *Isn't there more to life than working? When does the fun begin?*

I vowed I wouldn't miss out on fun, and other meaningful things in life, by working all the time the way Dad had. As the company grew and my role grew with it, I began to think about what really excited me. It wasn't being a veterinarian or a successful businessman, it was challenging myself in the great outdoors.

Over the years, I had tried a range of adventures. Parachuting. Mountain climbing. Scuba-diving. Motorcycling. Each of them offered its own unique, heart-pounding excitement. But none of those captured my imagination in a truly lifechanging way. The one that stuck was cave diving, which I first discovered in 1997.

Cave diving

Like Harry, I took a beginner's course. Unlike Harry, I took to cave diving immediately. I went on a few small dives to gain experience, then my instructor and friend, Steve Sturgeon, invited me to join his cave-diving expedition to Vanuatu. I was a novice. For the first time I experienced the thrill of seeing something that no human had ever seen before. I loved every second of the diving and vowed to do more.

Everything about it appealed to me. Descending from sunshine into darkness. Managing what seemed to me very complex diving equipment. Squeezing through narrow passages and countless twists and turns. Paddling across still, open pools. Discovering amazing geological formations. Trying to figure out where the water flow was coming from. Overcoming rapid currents, bracing temperatures, sometimes zero visibility, whereas at other times, the water was amazingly clear. Carefully unspooling the line that would guide us safely back home. Plus whatever nature threw our way. On that trip Steve had a serious accident during a dive and had to be evacuated by charter flight back to Australia, so I was also introduced to the dangers of cave diving. But I was determined to pursue it.

The day I returned from one dive trip, I began planning another, if I hadn't started already. I learned deep diving in abandoned mines in the Goldfields region of Western Australia and made many visits to the Nullarbor Plain, an area famous for its beautiful and extensive limestone cave systems. The diving was spectacular and so was the camaraderie. Cave divers, as I would discover, are a predictably colourful and strong-willed lot.

I grew fascinated by Cocklebiddy Cave, one of the Nullarbor Plain's crown jewels and at one time the longest known cave dive in the world. Cave divers had been exploring Cocklebiddy for years, but I believe we were the first to dive it to the end in one continuous trip, which took a little over thirty hours.

By then, I was totally hooked. I *had* to explore these caves. They are utterly virgin territory. Apart from space exploration, which is a little beyond my budget, what other outdoor activity promises that sort of adventure?

The only problem for me was finding the time.

Business or pleasure

As the years rolled along, my day job had become even more demanding. We had merged with an Adelaide-based company to form the Australian Animal Hospitals group, with fifteen practices in Perth and four in Adelaide. I was very proud of all that we achieved.

Along the way, I had met my life partner, Heather Endall. Heather is highly accomplished and a force of nature in her own right. She had already had a long and successful career before she joined Vetwest in an executive role in 2013.

The future was looking very bright. But by 2017, I had been running the company for twenty-four years, and I wanted more time for other things in my life, especially cave diving and aviation, my latest adventure. I had bought a helicopter and an aeroplane and enjoyed flying both of them and learning about a new field of endeavour. So in January of that year, I left the office for the final time and retired as a veterinarian.

I didn't think I'd look back late in life and wish I'd spent more time in the office. There were so many places I still had to fly to, so many caves just begging to be explored.

3

TEAMING UP

CRAIG

Cave divers

All the serious cave divers in the world could probably fit in a small fleet of buses, and the global community of first-rate cave divers is even smaller. Most of us know each other. Or we know *of* each other, and who the solid divers are. Cave divers tend to be individualistic and self-reliant, the kind of people who like to push themselves hard and can tolerate physical risk. Inside a cave, you are responsible for your own safety and survival. But cave diving is still very much a team sport, one for people who've always hated playing on teams. We're often together in remote locales for many days on end. We need help lugging equipment. We need people who can put up with the endless stories about our dive trips. We rely on each other's technical skill and support, starting with the crucial diver who lays the guide line that will steer us in and out of the cave.

When you're a hundred metres below the ground in a fast-moving current with zero visibility and nothing above your head but solid rock, your life really is in the hands of the friends you're diving with, especially the one who is your diving partner.

Diving with Harry

Harry and I had heard about each other before we'd ever met. By 2005, we'd both been diving a while. He'd started before I had, but I'd stuck with it and he'd drifted away while he finished med school, married and started having kids. In 2006, I went on a trip to Kija Blue, a massive, azure-blue sinkhole in the remote Kimberley region of arid north-western Australia, and Harry came along.

Kija Blue was stunning. Harry and I became fast friends.

I may tolerate risk more than Harry does, but we both see the world in very similar ways. When we're trying to solve a problem, we may start with opposite points of view, but we respect each other's opinions, and can always reach a conclusion together. These bonds are forged in the dark.

But our personalities could hardly be any more different. Harry is louder and more talkative and loves making fun of himself. I am more stubborn, more focused and more single-mindedly intense. I'd say we're both pretty smart. I think Harry would say: 'My first impression of Craig was that he takes a bit of time to get to know. You have to earn his friendship. Craig doesn't suffer fools. If he thinks something is unjust, he will fight it as long and hard as he can.'

Harry and I shared an obsession with the Pearse Resurgence in New Zealand's Kahurangi National Park – deep, cold and dangerous. On one nine-hour dive, my 194-metre descent broke the depth record by 12 metres, a record previously held by Harry. Year after year, we leapfrogged each other's Pearse Resurgence dives: 207 metres, 221 metres, then finally 229 metres for Harry. We loved working out how to safely push our personal limits and the limits of physiology.

For Harry and me, cave diving has always been a hobby, sometimes an obsession, but never a job. The records and recognition are a by-product of going out in the bush and doing our thing, not the reason for doing it. We do it to challenge ourselves, and we do it for fun.

Danger

Cave diving may or may not be the world's most dangerous sport. Hundreds of divers have perished in flooded caves, including some of the best. Diving in a cave tugs at some of the deepest human fears – drowning, darkness, isolation, being trapped. Cave diving is as different from regular scuba diving as scuba is from snorkelling. It's far more dangerous, since so many more things can go wrong: silt-outs; floods; rockfalls; losing your line; getting lost in the darkness and running out of air. Cave divers must be prepared for any and all eventualities and must never forget one life-or-death fact: panic and mistakes kill many more divers than geological surprises and equipment mishaps combined, which is why a big part of learning to cave dive is learning to keep your cool, no matter what.

And that can be tough. It's hard to communicate down there. Panic thrives underground. It's dark. It's confusing. It's confined. Rock is notoriously unforgiving. When you crash into it, it doesn't give. Passageways can be stubbornly narrow and hard to navigate. The pressure increases with the depth. And a diver in trouble can't swim through rock straight to the surface for a breath of fresh air. The only way out is the way you came in.

Many of the world's most exciting caves don't look like much from the outside. But that out-of-the-way sinkhole or nondescript pond could easily extend kilometres underground, concealing an intricate array of underwater corridors and dramatic rock formations. And caves aren't just physically stunning. They are often powerful preservers of the past, time capsules that contain some of the deepest secrets of our planet and how it was formed.

Cave-diving pioneers

The earliest cave divers didn't use any equipment at all. They climbed into the water, held their breath, and swam as far as they could. Frenchman Norbert Casteret, a World War I veteran with an unquenchable thirst for adventure, made a bold free dive in 1923 in the Grotte de Montespan, where he discovered prehistoric drawings on a distant wall and secured his place as a hero to generations of cave divers to come. Norbert would tuck a candle in his oilskin cap to light the darkness of the sump, a drowned passageway. No one could possibly discount the bravery – or lung capacity – of such fearless pioneers.

Technology developed slowly from the first breathing machines, to oxygen cylinders, frogman suits and other wartime equipment, to the aqualung, invented in 1943.

By 1960, modern wetsuits offered a much-improved mix of buoyancy and insulation. Side-mounted cylinders made it easier to move underwater, as cave divers squeezed their bodies through narrower and narrower openings. Visibility was improved, too, with more intense helmet-mounted lights. Fins extended divers' range even further.

By the mid-1960s, organised cave diving was beginning to spread around the world, especially to Australia, New Zealand and the USA.

The rise of professional instruction pushed safety as priority number one, and cave-diving equipment was finally being standardised. Following the 'rule of thirds' became the norm: a third of your air on the way into the cave, a third for the trip out and the final third as a safety reserve. Carrying more than one cylinder, each with an independent demand valve, also became standard practice, meaning that a diver in trouble would always have a backup. These basics would save countless lives over the years. Violating them would prove fatal time and time again.

Technical diving revolution

Such was the state of cave diving when Harry and I showed up in the 1990s. Divers had made great advances. So had the gear. But the possibilities were about to explode again with the arrival of the so-called technical diving revolution. Truly, the fun had only just begun.

When Harry and I started diving, people had begun experimenting with different mixes of oxygen, nitrogen and helium to extend the dives and make them safer. Rebreathers are manually or electronically controlled devices that allow you to breathe the same air repeatedly by adding oxygen and removing carbon dioxide from your inhaled air, allowing you to dive deeper and stay longer. The masks and the fins hadn't changed much, but the exposure suits, as we call them, were always improving. Wetsuits, drysuits, new concepts and new materials. There is a suit – often many suits – for almost any dive.

Why dive in a cave?

But why would anyone want to dive in a cave?

I used to say: 'If you need to ask the question, you wouldn't understand the answer.' If it doesn't call to you, I probably can't convince you to love it.

Curiosity is part of the appeal. If I'm walking through the bush and I see a hole in the ground, I really need to know: 'How deep is that hole? Does it go straight down or veer to the side? Where does the water in it come from?' For Harry, it's about exploration, but it's also about bringing back video and images to share with others.

Challenge is another part of cave diving's appeal. If anyone could do it, it wouldn't be nearly so much fun. Cave diving can be logistically complicated, physically gruelling and potentially dangerous – all the things that cavers love.

Technical fascination is part of it too. Divers tend to be technically minded people. We are constantly testing new equipment – how to prepare it, how to repair it and how to improve on it.

But the biggest attraction in cave diving, I believe, is the excitement of exploration, the desire to see things no one has ever seen and of possibly discovering something new.

Agnes

Of all the dives Harry and I have taken together, the one that prepared us best for Thailand was our saddest dive of all.

Agnes Milowka was a rising star of cave diving and a great friend of ours, an extremely talented and self-assured young Australian diver. Born in Poland, Agnes had moved to Melbourne as a child and studied maritime archaeology at Flinders University. She had done a lot of wreck diving, then discovered the thrill of cave diving and shot right up the ranks. 'I dream about caves,' she said early on.

Still in her twenties, she made amazing discoveries in Australia and the USA. She caused some controversy because she would sneak into the caves by herself after work. But that was Agnes, pushing fast and hard. On an expedition to Cocklebiddy Cave in Western Australia, she reached the midpoint of the line I had laid in 2008, giving her the record for the longest cave dive in Australia for a female.

'Don't rush things. Just be careful,' several of us urged her. But she was young and didn't give much thought to her own mortality.

Agnes worked with *National Geographic* and the Discovery Channel. She was a stunt diver on James Cameron's 3D diving film, *Sanctum*, which she described on her website as the story of what can happen when a dive 'goes terribly wrong'. 'Inside a cave system,' she wrote, 'the line between life and death is a fine one, which naturally makes for thrilling adventure.' Agnes made a few comments that, frankly, worried Harry and me. 'You'd have to be stupid to die in Mount Gambier in those simple caves,' she told us one day, which was maybe a little insensitive to the twelve or thirteen people who had died there over the years.

But we loved Agnes. Everybody did.

Fast-forward to February 2011. The caves of Piccaninnie Ponds, twenty kilometres west of Mount Gambier. When Harry surfaced, he was told that someone in the group hadn't come out of nearby Tank Cave. Tank Cave is only around fifteen metres deep, but it's a complex maze with eight kilometres of interwoven tunnels and tight restrictions. He had a sinking feeling: *It's going to be Agnes.*

As well as we could piece together later, Agnes had bowled into a hole leading to a new passage about 600 metres from the entrance and kept going, squeezing through some extremely narrow openings. She was small, and famous for pushing through tight, restricted places. At one point she had taken off one of her cylinders to push herself further in. That's a risky manoeuvre. You've dropped your extra gas supply. If anything goes wrong with your other tank, you're in serious trouble.

Going further into the cave, she'd turned around and got lost in the silt. She never made it out.

It was a group effort to find Agnes's body. It looked like Agnes had still been fighting right to the end. When the gas ran out, she had returned to within three metres of her other tank, but she was pointing in the wrong direction, blinded by silt.

I arrived from Perth the next day after Harry called me in to help. For three days, working in buddy pairs, we and other divers dug out the cave to reach her body and retrieve her gear. Harry did the last dive, bringing Agnes's body out to a spot where I was waiting, about five metres back. From there Harry led us out. I followed, drawing Agnes along behind me.

As we moved along this tiny, flat tunnel, Harry floated up off the floor a little and ended up in a sort of blind alcove in the roof of the cave. Neither of us could see anything, and I had no idea what was happening. I kept moving forwards, squashing Harry from behind, trapping him, as he tried to work out why the tunnel had just stopped. A very simple error could have been a major problem. Harry told me later he really had to fend off rising panic there. That's a risk and often a reality in any rescue or recovery.

Agnes's loss was a tragedy for us, but her memory lives on in awards and at least three geological features named in her memory.

'There is no greater feeling in the world than finding a passage that no one ever in the history of the world has seen before,' Agnes said in one of her many YouTube videos.

'To me those risks are worth it, because the rewards are worth it.'

I just wish she were still around to enjoy more of them. She was only twenty-nine years old.

4

CAVE CHAOS

HARRY

The possibility of our going to Thailand was suggested as early as 27 June, four days after the team members disappeared. That Wednesday morning, the captain of the New South Wales Cave Rescue Squad called to say the Australian government had asked him to 'chase up cave divers' who could help in Thailand. 'Any ideas?' he asked. 'Are you available? Know anyone suitable?'

I answered promptly. 'Craig and I could be available . . . Is it a recovery or a rescue?' No one knew at that point, five days before the boys were found, and that's the first question you've always got to ask. 'Craig is okay to go,' he told me – he'd already asked.

Itching to help

As we waited to hear more, I got a message later that Wednesday from Ben Reymenants, a Belgian diver living in Thailand. A big crowd was gathering, he said, and he was making his way swiftly into the cave.

'Any excuse to pop over, mate!' I nudged him.

Ben answered noncommittally. 'Thanks, I'll let you know. Still raining, water is muddy and rising.'

I heard from Ben again Wednesday night:

> I have two Thai guys that went in. Rick Stanton and 2 other British cave explorers arrived. Thai navy is pumping out water and trying to divert a waterfall which fills up the cave, but there's a very tight restriction the divers can't get past with their back mount, so it's side mount only. Focus is now on getting someone in to check if they're alive and sending supplies until the water drops.

The big news was that Rick Stanton was on the scene. If Rick and his British dive partners were involved, the rescue operation was almost certain to become more professional, pronto. Rick tends to be followed by a trail of accolades. *The greatest . . . the most respected . . . the most experienced.* Rick had been involved in more rescues and body recoveries than most. Put it like this: if you're stuck in a cave, you want him on the scene – and not just because of the diving records he holds. He's at least as proud of his 'Hero of the Year' awards from the West Midland Fire Service. A firefighter for twenty-five years, he has the skills to make a difference and rescue is in his blood. If he could make a difference for the stranded Wild Boars, the 57-year-old diver would surely be hailed a hero again. But I also sensed an imminent clash between Rick and Ben. Two strong personalities – international legend versus local hotshot – both of them now at Tham Luang cave.

Ben wrote to me again on Thursday morning:

> Unsure how to transport 12 kids over 1km distance in zero viz against flow. They can't swim and never dove.

The *can't swim* part would turn out later not to be true. Sitting at home in Adelaide, I got the feeling there was a Ben-team and a Rick-team, and they were working independently. But I was happy to keep up the dialogue with Ben. 'Give a call if you want to chat,' I wrote back to him. 'We have done some practice like this with FFMs, switch blocks and QDs' – full face masks and devices for switching between different air tanks.

At the same time, I had also contacted Rick and John, offering encouragement and reminding them how willing Craig and I were to assist. 'Hi guys,' I wrote,

> If you manage to get to these guys, they will likely need medical assistance and you will need a team of divers to take turns to baby sit them while an extraction plan comes together, which may take some time. Craig and I are happy to provide any assistance to your team if required. All the best, Harry.

Barely an hour later, I heard back from Rick. 'Thanks for the offer of help,' he wrote. 'You've thought of the issues involved. Struggling to progress against the current and water unlikely to recede until end of monsoon season.'

'All sounds v sad,' I answered.

'Above statement best kept in relative confidence until the news is slowly released,' Rick cautioned, already noticing that the media coverage sounded far more optimistic than things appeared. 'There may still be other successful options in the meantime.'

Confusion at the cave site

The increasing free-for-all at the cave site – too many people, too little organisation, too much media – was undermining the mission, Rick said. 'We're pulling out as there's nothing we can do,' he wrote in his latest message to me.

'At least you saved some rescuers,' I said, trying to offer consolation. I was referring to the four water workers that Rick and John had found stranded in the cave on an earlier dive. I asked about the possibility of alternative entrances to the cave.

'Not much chance but certainly worth pursuing,' Rick answered. 'We think they fled a flood from the southern passage where they were headed,' he wrote. 'Encountered a sump at Monks Junction halting their exit. Then it's whether they were able to retreat upstream to Pattaya Beach, but I suspect not as there are U-bends that would fill.'

'Might be kinder if they couldn't escape it,' I wrote. This was how low everything had sunk.

'I agree,' Rick answered. 'Vern, our local expert, who's been correct so far, says it may not be until Dec or Jan until U-bends will have drained.'

'Yuck.'

And that, right there, could have been the end of it all. The Thai military, with almost no cave-diving experience, could have taken over all future efforts to locate and rescue the boys with help from Ben. And Rick Stanton, the greatest and most respected cave diver on earth, could have packed up his guys and his gear and grabbed the next flight to Heathrow.

Progress

It is extremely fortunate that didn't happen, especially for the twelve junior soccer players and their young assistant coach, huddled somewhere in the darkness of Tham Luang cave. When I heard back from Rick on Sunday afternoon, he said things had improved slightly:

> JV and I reached the Monks Junction so there is now 800m of continuous rope beyond 3rd chamber. 500m to reach Pattaya beach from there. Much more airspaces than expected so passage beyond 350m is mainly canals with many short dives. Water dropping, 2 m. We have a two-day window to achieve something.

'Great news,' I answered. 'I really wish I could be there in case they are alive and need medical attention.'

'They have Special Forces doctors ready to dive in on LAR rebreathers and live 3 months in the cave with the boys,' Rick said. Then he added: 'Needless to say this could all go very wrong when it rains. This is beyond our level, we're here as pathfinders.'

'Ah, okay,' I answered. 'Glad they have a plan. Keen to use my skills!'

It was the next afternoon, Monday, that Rick and John located the Wild Boars on a muddy ledge just past Pattaya Beach.

By the next day, seven Thai Navy SEALs, including Thai Army doctor Pak Loharnshoon, had made the arduous dive in. Pak and three others vowed to remain with the boys and the coach as long as it took to get everyone out.

All that sent a blast of optimism through everyone. The media believed that now the boys had been located the rest would be straightforward. *How hard could it be to get them out?* I knew that exactly the opposite was likely to be true. However hard it had been finding them in the cave, getting them out of there was a far bigger challenge.

I texted Rick first thing on Thursday morning, and he replied, 'There's stuff to talk about. They are not being dived out by Thai navy. Could you sedate someone and dive them out??'

Rescue options

That was the first time Rick mentioned sedation to me. He couldn't be serious, I thought. *Diving a sedated child underwater? Through the narrow constrictions of a flooded cave?*

'What do you think about diving them out?' I replied. 'Sedation not an option.'

Time was running out for Craig and me. 'I would still come if you thought I could help,' I said to Rick. 'Leaving for Nullarbor in 24 hrs though.'

We'd been very excited about our trip before Thailand came up. The Nullarbor is dotted with some utterly awe-inspiring caves. But we'd be out of range of wi-fi or phone service, so we'd know nothing about what was happening in Thailand.

'Harry,' Craig said as we packed our trucks for the long drives the next morning, 'one day we'll be involved in a great cave rescue. But this won't be the one.'

Finding the boys earned Rick and John plenty of trust and respect. I hoped they would soon be granted more influence over the rescue planning.

By now, there was no shortage of rescue ideas floating around, but neither Rick nor John nor Craig nor I had any more confidence in most of these schemes. That the cave could be effectively drained now that the rainy season had started. That the mountain drillers could aim perfectly and drill a hole to the exact spot where the boys were. Rick wasn't counting on any of it.

Perhaps the most extraordinary ideas came from tech billionaire Elon Musk. On Wednesday, Musk announced on Twitter that he was 'happy to help' rescue the boys in Thailand, adding that he had ordered his top engineers to come up with a creative plan, or three.

The first was a nylon tube that could be inflated like a birthday party bouncy castle to create an underwater air tunnel. The kids, he said, could then walk out of the cave, high and dry, without needing to dive at all. When divers on the scene pointed out the many shortcomings of his plan, Musk had another proposal.

A 'kid-size submarine'.

The minisub, he said, would be made from a metal cylinder from a spaceship, large enough to hold a boy or two. He said he would begin testing the vessel in a swimming pool in Los Angeles, with divers front and back, and personally deliver it to Thailand.

In case the minisub could not fit through the narrow openings of the cave, Musk also asked engineers to build blow-up escape pods, which were designed, made-up and tested in one day before being flown to Thailand.

It is fair to say that no prominent cave divers greeted Musk's ideas with much enthusiasm.

Rick, Craig, John and I were equally sceptical of another popular idea: just leave the boys inside with food, water and other necessities until they could be safely walked out at the end of the rainy season. Trying to sustain thirteen young people deep inside a cave for months on end would be a medical nightmare. What would happen when they started getting dysentery? How would the site stay clean? Where would they go to the toilet? How would they stay dry and warm? What would you do with all the dead bodies, as the boys succumbed one at a time? The issues were insurmountable. In Rick's mind – and in mine – you'd only be replacing a fast death with a slow one.

Then, there was the idea of diving them out, after some brief instruction. But a crash scuba course could never prepare a soccer team of eleven- to sixteen-year-olds for such a dive. Hadn't it just taken a team of exceptional Navy SEALs with years of diving experience six gruelling hours to dive *in*?

Sedation?

Rick kept returning to some questions he was obviously wrestling with. *What if the young people were anaesthetised?*

I understood why Rick was drawn to sedation – it solved the problem of the boys panicking. Panic is a powerful human reflex, nearly impossible to control. On a long underwater journey, flailing arms, violent movements, the yanking of hoses and face masks could prove deadly for the boys and possibly even the expert divers escorting them.

'You've sedated thousands of patients over the years, young and old,' Rick said to me at one point.

'Yes, but never once in a cave.'

Sedating these children, I explained, would involve unique risks, starting with the most basic one: how on earth could you dive unconscious children through a long and dangerous cave without drowning them? Diving requires the active participation of the diver. What happens when water leaks into the face mask? What happens when an air hose fails? What would you do when the drug wore off? How would you know what dose to administer? It sounded almost as reckless as leaving the boys inside the cave.

But Rick kept reminding me that we weren't hunting for the perfect solution, only the best one.

I sent one last message to Rick Stanton before Craig and I headed off the grid. Little did I expect, that would be the message that landed.

'I think we could use you,' Rick said finally. 'And if the issue of sedation doesn't go away, you're the guys to do it.'

Craig and I were going to Thailand at last.

5

LOST BOYS

CRAIG

Harry and I had never dived in Tham Luang cave, but we'd been inside caves like it, and we knew many of the divers engaged in the search or who would soon be flying in to participate in the rescue. We also understood just how daunting this mission would be. Most cave-diving rescues end as body recoveries. That's just a fact. Almost all the divers seemed to agree: these precious young people were highly unlikely to come out of that cave alive.

How it began

The trouble had started, as trouble often does, in the most mundane way imaginable. It had been a humid, cloudy Saturday in the far-northern Mae Sai district of Thailand's Chiang Rai province, near the Thai–Myanmar border. The boys of the Moo Pa ('Wild Boars') youth soccer program had just finished a weekend practice club friendly. After coming off the field, a dozen of the young players, aged eleven to sixteen, decided to make one last stop before heading home. One of the boys, Pheeraphat Sompiengjai, known by his nickname 'Night', was celebrating his sixteenth birthday that day, making him the oldest player on the team. Night's parents had a bright-yellow SpongeBob SquarePants cake waiting for him at home. But the boys wanted to hold their own small celebration.

They rode their bikes from the practice field through rice paddies and forested hills to Tham Luang cave, about twenty minutes away. Their young assistant coach, Ekkapol Chantawong ('Coach Ekk'), agreed to come along. The boys stopped on the way for some snacks and juices. Outside the cave, they carefully lined up their bikes against a rail, dropped their backpacks in the dirt and traded their soccer shoes for thongs and sneakers. Excited, they hiked inside together.

'Just a short visit,' Coach Ekk cautioned. 'Then, everyone must go home.'

Some people thought the coach's decision was reckless or worse. But most of the players had been to the cave – it's a local tourist attraction – and had even conducted initiation rituals inside one of the deeper chambers, writing the names of new team members on a flat limestone wall. Until the monsoon season arrived each summer, a short visit to the cave wouldn't spark any alarm at all, despite the sign at the mouth of the cave in English and Thai: 'DANGER! FROM JULY – NOVEMBER THE CAVE IS FLOODING SEASON.' But July was still eight days away, and although it had been raining on and off for the past three days, there was no sign of flooding at the mouth of the cave. The boys, most still dressed in their soccer jerseys and shorts, with a few cheap headlights to illuminate the way, advanced through the first chamber and hiked deeper inside.

In the rich folklore of northern Thailand, there are many stories about these cloud-swathed mountains and the caves that snake beneath them. The Tham Luang – Khun Nam Nang Non, as this underground system is officially called, means 'The Great Cave and Water Source of the Sleeping Lady Mountain'.

It is said that in ancient times a beautiful princess fell in love with a stableboy and became pregnant by him. Knowing their love was forbidden, the young couple fled to the cave to hide. When the stableboy left in search of food, he was caught by the king's army and killed. The princess then stabbed herself and bled to death in the cave. As legend has it, the surrounding mountains took the shape of the princess's body and her blood became the water that flows through the cave. To this day, her spirit is said to inhabit the cave, controlling all who enter.

It took a couple of hours for the boys' parents to grow concerned. By then, the rain had begun to fall again. This time, it was hard and steady and didn't let up. Around 7 p.m., as darkness was falling, Wild Boars head coach Nopparat Kanthawong checked his phone and found more than twenty missed calls and voice messages from parents worried that their sons had not come home. Nopparat dialled his assistant, Coach Ekk, as well as several of the missing boys. No one answered. Eventually, though, the head coach reached one of his other players, thirteen-year-old Songpol Kanthawong, his nephew.

'Do you know where Ekk is?' the coach asked frantically. 'Do you know where the boys are?'

'They went to the cave,' Songpol answered. He had planned to go along, he said, but his mother had called and insisted he return home with the motor scooter he had ridden to soccer practice that day. She needed it for work. Reluctantly, Songpol had farewelled his friends.

The head coach drove straight to the cave, where he spotted his players' bikes and backpacks strewn on what was now a muddy path. He realised Ekk and the boys must still be inside the cave and called the authorities immediately. He then alerted the worried parents, who started arriving soon after the police and paramedics, joined by some Thai soldiers, then park rangers. No one knew what to do if the Wild Boars were lost somewhere in the twisted depths of Tham Luang cave.

Though the first part of the cave was dry, park rangers came upon a T-junction where the water had risen too high for them to pass. All anyone could hope was that the boys hadn't been washed away in the rising floodwaters – that they'd found a dry ledge to wait out these dicey hours.

Help arrives

By the next morning, the crowd outside the cave had begun to swell with a fresh wave of Thai national police officers, military personnel and concerned local residents, all eager to help. They joined the first responders and anxious relatives who had stayed all night. Among the newcomers was Vern Unsworth, a British caver based in Chiang Rai, an hour's drive south of the cave.

News crews gathered, their satellite trucks parked along the road to the cave. Slowly, details about the boys began creeping into the media, along with photos from their Facebook pages and from classmates' mobile phones. Mark was the smallest, though not the youngest. Titan, the youngest, was deathly afraid of the dark. Dom's mother ran a clothing stand in the Mae Sai market. Five of the boys attended Mae Sai Prasitsart School. The Wild Boars were coming to life in the public's mind, moving from a generic group of Thai children – 'the boys' – to individuals with distinct personalities and special family circumstances. Coach Ekk and three of the boys, Adul, Mark and Tee, were not actually Thai citizens. Though born in Thailand, they came from ethnic groups who for generations have moved across borders in the remote hills of China, Myanmar, Laos and Thailand. Like half a million others in Thailand, these so-called stateless people are denied many of the basic rights of citizenship.

Ekk's story was especially tragic. In 2003, when he was just ten years old, an epidemic swept through his tiny village, killing his mother, father and seven-year-old brother and sparing only him. A sad and lonely boy, Ekk was taken in by relatives, who sent him to a Buddhist temple, where he trained to be a monk. He shaved his head, wore saffron robes, learned to meditate and studied the Tripitaka, the Mahayana sutras and the Tibetan Book of the Dead, the three major Buddhist texts.

Ekk moved out of the temple to care for his ageing grandmother, and that's when he became the Wild Boars' assistant coach. He loved the boys, everyone agreed, often looking after them when their parents were busy or away. None of the parents seemed to blame the coach at all. 'I would be so much more worried if Coach Ekk wasn't with them,' one of the fathers said. 'He will do whatever he must to keep them safe.'

Outside the cave, fear for the boys' safety mounted. 'My son, come out,' cried Titan's mother. 'I am waiting for you here.'

'Please hurry and come home,' wailed another, whose son, Biw, was the team's goalie. 'My son, let's go home together.'

The mother of a boy named Dom began to weep as soon as she recognised her son's bike and soccer bag. 'My heart is gone!' she cried.

One of the fathers was obviously torn. 'I am not sure if we will find them today if it keeps raining,' he said. 'But I asked for all God's wishes. I am certain that they will survive.'

Several red-eyed parents gathered in a sombre prayer ceremony led by an elderly saffron-robed monk, accompanied by the slow, haunting beat of a small drum. In this region, beliefs and traditions are heavily influenced by Buddhism, animism and Brahmin traditions. 'We believe that all places have guardian spirits, places like mountains, caves and houses,' as one local woman explained. 'We may not see them, but they can see us. So we need to respect them.' Someone set up a simple shrine to Jao Mae Nang Non, as the Sleeping Lady is known, and people began to leave offerings of soft drinks, boiled eggs, fruit and desserts. No one could explain why the Sleeping Lady would trap the boys in the cave, but once she was fully satisfied, it was widely agreed, the youngsters would be found. Classmates of the boys held a group prayer session, singing songs of encouragement, folding paper cranes and posting hopeful messages on their Facebook pages. A sense of real community – or was it shared grief and terror? – began to take hold. Tents were brought in for the distraught parents, who vowed to remain at the cave until their sons were found. As the rain kept falling, the tents were not nearly enough to keep anyone dry.

Over the next days, more military personnel arrived, including Royal Thai Navy SEALs, and offers of assistance poured in from Australia, China, Britain, Belgium, Scandinavia and America. A team of United States Air Force pararescuers were said to be coming. As the media horde continued to grow, Chiang Rai governor Narongsak Osottanakorn, who holds degrees in geology and engineering, took personal charge of the scene. There was still no clear rescue plan. But the straight-talking governor began to issue orders and hold regular briefings, and brought some basic order to the chaos of the cave site. One of his first acts was to separate the families from the media.

'Whatever part you play in the mission,' he said to rescuers and responders at the scene, 'I ask you to think of the boys as your own children. That is how much we care about them. We won't abandon them. We are in this fully.'

Calling all cave divers

As news of the boys' plight spread, the international cave-diving community was also springing into action. Not surprisingly, the people closest to Tham Luang got there first. Vern Unsworth got a call the morning after the boys were lost and came right over. The boys were so lucky he did.

Vern had learned caving as a boy in the dales of Yorkshire, England. Now, he lived part of the year in Chiang Rai, an hour's drive south of the cave. He'd spent years exploring the cave, tracing its narrow passages and blind turn-offs, taking notes and measurements, numbering the chambers and making himself thoroughly at home. He'd gone further and deeper than anyone before him. He spoke to Governor Osottanakorn and local officials. He warned about the dangers of thoughtlessly rushing in. He explained the layout of the cave and shared his personal maps. Vern even offered his best-guess prediction about where the boys would likely be found. He said they'd most likely head for a section called Pattaya Beach, a big sandbank, about two and a half kilometres in, named for Thailand's famous tourist beach.

'We need people with diving experience,' Vern told the Thai authorities. Not the Thai Army or Navy, or even the elite Thai Navy SEALs, who were trained in combat diving and maritime counterterrorism but not in cave diving. The SEALs had plenty of heart, but they weren't used to squeezing their bodies through openings no wider than their hips or swimming through swirling water the colour of instant coffee, let alone swimming beneath hundreds of metres of rock where there was no escape to the surface if trouble appeared. Rescuing these children was a job for people like the veteran sump divers associated with the British Cave Rescue Council, adventurers who felt entirely at home in constricted, low-visibility, underwater caves. The SEALs and other Thai troops could provide valuable support, Vern said. 'But this is a race against time. Only world-class divers will save these kids.'

But by Tuesday afternoon, none of the Thai officials had acted on his pleas. The SEALs and others kept diving, but they hadn't found the boys. The rain had let up a bit, but the sky was still cloudy, and no one could say when the next storm might blow in. As far as Vern was concerned, now was the last chance for action. It was literally do-or-die.

The SEALs were getting some help from a well-known cave diver who had also shown up at the scene. Ben Reymenants was a 45-year-old Belgian who owned a dive shop and diving school on the southern Thai resort island of Phuket. Ben was a media-savvy businessman-diver with a brash personal style. Harry and I knew him well from a couple of diving trips we'd done together, including one to Thailand's Song Hong, a sinkhole we had dived to 196 metres. Very few people specialise in this deep diving, and Ben is one of them.

Ben laid a considerable length of line inside Tham Luang cave in the first few days, diving in very high water flow and very poor visibility, pushing beyond the range of the less-experienced SEALs. These were risky dives, as Ben recounted in his media and social-media reports. But Vern Unsworth had received a call from Rob Harper, a caving friend who'd left Thailand for England the week before. Rob mentioned that he knew two of the greatest cave divers on earth. Those were the kinds of people Vern had in mind.

Around 9 p.m. on Tuesday, Vern was called into a meeting with politicians and the governor. He grabbed a pen and wrote a short note:

> *Time is running out! 1) Rob Harper; 2) Rick Stanton MBE; 3) John Volanthen – they're the world's best cave divers. Please contact them through UK Embassy ASAP.*

'What do you want me to do?' the minister asked after reading Vern's note, sounding like a man in an uncomfortable squeeze.

'Call them now,' said Vern. 'Here's my phone.'

Rob Harper was in his pyjamas lying in bed. As a veterinary surgeon he often worked at night, but he was fully awake now and eager to help in any way he could.

The British Cave Rescue Council handled the logistics. Rob, Rick Stanton and John Volanthen were on the late-night flight from Heathrow to Bangkok. Finally, things were about to change.

Rick, John and Rob

When Rick, John and Rob arrived at the cave site, Vern took them to meet the diving supervisor, a stern Thai military officer at the mouth of the cave. His men had been pushing themselves to the edge of exhaustion day and night. What could these two middle-aged hobbyists from Britain possibly achieve that his fit, young Navy special operators could not?

Rick and John were the most experienced cave divers by far, but they had no rank or authority, and it took until late on Wednesday before they were given permission to enter the cave.

The Brits quickly gathered their gear and strode to the mouth of the cave. 'We've got a job to do' was all John would say as he and Rick brushed past the reporters.

The initial dives through the first chambers were tougher than they expected. Strong, swirling rapids of dirty brown water made accurate navigation impossible. They pointed their noses into the strongest flow and groped forwards. Just reaching chamber 3, the large dry chamber that was to become the advanced staging post for future dives, was tremendously difficult. When they finally reached it, they had their first shock.

They were appalled to find themselves face to face with four Thai men in orange overalls, employees of the Thai Well Water Association, including association president Surapin Chaichompoo. They had been part of a civilian work crew trying to pump water out of the cave. After hours of gruelling effort, they took a nap in a quiet corner of chamber 3. When they woke, they were trapped by rising water. Everyone else had evacuated. No one seemed to notice these four had been left behind. The British divers had no choice but to temporarily abandon their search for the Wild Boars and rescue the four workers.

Since the British divers and Thai labourers shared no common language, Rick and John used hand signals to explain that they would be escorted through the ten-metre sump connecting chambers 3 and 2. The dive was shallow, but it was tight and made more so by the clutter of cables and pipes that had already been laid into the cave. Rick and John took turns, using each other's masks and cylinders to shuttle the workers through.

On Monday, 2 July, nine days after the boys disappeared, Rick and John swam back into chamber 3. It was large enough and dry enough to become a combination warehouse, dorm room and forward operating base from which to launch deeper explorations. Other divers, including the awesome lads from the Australian Federal Police, had been ferrying in air tanks and additional equipment. Military MREs – meals ready to eat – and cartons of bottled water had also been carried in, enough to sustain a long stay. Many of the Thai Navy SEALs brought in sleeping-bags and space blankets.

Rick Stanton and John Volanthen kept pressing forwards into the darkness, laying more line and searching each new section of cave for any signs of life. Every time they surfaced into an air space, they removed their masks and sniffed the air. If the boys were here, dead or alive, they'd smell them; smell is always one of the experienced diver's greatest assets. But they found nothing. Finally, they reached Pattaya Beach, the flat, sandy area where Vern had predicted the boys might be found. But there was no sign of them.

Found

The divers swam on. About 300 metres past Pattaya Beach, they reached an air space, lifted their heads and removed their masks. They couldn't see anything, but they sure smelled something. What was it? Excrement? Death? They expected to swim through the long canal and bump into the floating bodies of the children. It was a chilling moment.

But then the light from John's helmet lamp revealed something extraordinary: up to the right, several boys were stepping out of the darkness, walking down a sloping path from a muddy ledge, directly towards them.

What an exhilarating sight!

Rick started counting the boys, then John called out in English: 'How many of you?'

'Thirteen!' came the reply, also in English.

'Thirteen? Brilliant!'

And just 300 metres from the spot where Vern had said they would be.

If John and Rick were excited to see Coach Ekk and the boys, the feeling was more than mutual. The Wild Boars were thrilled when the British divers appeared. This was the moment they'd been desperately waiting for, one they feared might never come. In their excitement, many of the boys seemed to assume they would all be leaving the cave that day. So Rick and John had to explain that wasn't possible, but that they and other divers would definitely be back soon. Before saying goodbye, they left some lights and energy bars with the boys, and they captured the brief encounter on John's helmet-mounted video camera.

When the short video was posted on the Navy SEALs' Facebook page soon after they left the cave, it was the first real piece of good news in nine exhausting, excruciating, emotionally draining days. Hope and celebration erupted at the cave site, where the parents, classmates, rescuers and volunteers had grown so weary and discouraged. Then, happiness for the boys spread via the media all around the world, as some of the details of their underground captivity began to leak out.

They'd been sleeping on the ledge where Rick and John had found them without a single blanket to keep them warm. They'd been drinking the water that had flowed by them in the cave. They'd been without food for nine long days. They'd been wandering around a corner to relieve themselves. And yet in the video, they all sounded remarkably cheerful. The boys and the coach all flashed wonderful, happy smiles. They all looked healthy at first glance. Could things really have gone so well for them in Tham Luang cave? Rick and John could only report what they saw. And for now it was encouraging.

They're alive!

The boys and their young coach are alive!

But the good news didn't mean they would ever see their families and friends again. Or that they wouldn't die one day soon, two and a half kilometres from the rest of their lives. The cave was still flooded. Its passages were still narrow and treacherous. The boys and the coach still had no diving experience. The sky outside was still menacing and dark.

The chances of a successful outcome were still extraordinarily slim according to the most experienced cave divers.

There was no hint of this pessimism in the relentless media coverage. The discovery of the boys was being hailed as such a massive triumph, it felt almost rude to wonder out loud:

So what happens next?

Photos of the young players were everywhere, accompanied by their bare-bones biographies and their snappy nicknames. Mark. Mick. Pong. Tern. Titan. Here they were in their red, blue and black soccer jerseys, or in photos at school. Or pictured with their precious families, often with aching comments from their shell-shocked parents, who sounded exhilarated that the boys had been found but also devastated that no one seemed to know how to bring them home.

The calamity brought out the good in many people, including those who lived closest to the cave. Fresh volunteers kept appearing at the scene to cook meals, cut hair, clean toilets or transport people and equipment. An entire, instant town grew up with no real order or plan, just a lot of nice people trying to help, as the British were joined by a growing contingent of European divers and cavers, and the SEALs and Thai government officials figured out what to do next. Advice and ideas were pouring in from everywhere.

Giant pumps were moved into the front of the cave, their powerful sucking motors pulling millions of litres of water out of the cave every hour but straining to reduce the water level. Engineers tried to calculate the best spots to drill down to the boys, aiming to create a vertical escape route for the boys to climb or be lifted up somehow. Ben and the other diving instructors were constantly being asked if they could train children to dive out with tanks, masks and fins.

No ideas were rejected outright by the Thai authorities. How could they be? No one knew what might be the magic bullet. Elon Musk, the billionaire co-founder of PayPal whose next-generation tech firms included the automaker Tesla and space explorer SpaceX, was asking publicly how his engineers might play a role. Whichever schemes were ultimately adopted, they would all come to nothing when the rain fell once more, washing away Coach Ekk and the dozen Wild Boars.

Then the Royal Thai Navy SEALs made an extraordinary offer. They would send in a seven-man team, some of whom would stay with the coach and the boys, watching over them and caring for them until they were rescued. The SEAL team would be led by a legendary Thai Army medic, Dr Pak Loharnshoon, known as Dr Pak, who had been through the full SEAL training course and was known as a talented, charismatic special-forces combatant and doctor. With a few diving tips from Rick and John, Pak and the SEALs got up early the next morning and made what was for them an excruciating six-hour dive.

They found the water uncomfortably chilly. Several suffered from cramps along the way and had to rest. And the SEALs managed to consume most of the air in their tanks. They'd have to figure out later how to get the air they'd need to dive everyone out. It was nearly noon by the time the seven-man team reached the boys in chamber 9.

It turned out there was sufficient air for only three of the SEALs to dive out that day, leaving Pak and three others behind. 'Everyone can be relieved now, as the boys are in the good hands of Navy SEALs, who will take care of them all the time,' the commander told the media. 'It may be four months, one month or one week. There is no need to hurry. Safety is the priority. There will be constant food and medicine provided to the trapped footballers and a communication line to the outside world.'

Any communicating was done the old-fashioned way, by divers carrying messages back and forth. The British divers had taken in further supplies: lights and batteries, and meals ready-to-eat from the US Air Force pararescue team. But the SEAL team brought something else the players had been missing – outside companionship.

Now, the boys had the greatest babysitters ever!

II
GOING

6

HOME FRONT

HARRY

As the drama of the lost boys was unfolding in Thailand, we couldn't believe we were missing it. But you can't just show up in Thailand and start rescuing a bunch of stranded children, even if Rick Stanton asks you to come.

'So how do we make this happen?' I asked Rick. 'Are there any Australian government people there?' I thought my government might be able to negotiate with the Thai government.

'Yeah,' Rick said. 'Federal police and some diplomatic people.'

'Could you ask them to start the ball rolling? Because I wouldn't have a clue who to call in Australia.'

Rick promised to try.

Your people speak to my people

Within an hour, I got a call from Canberra. The man on the phone said he was from DFAT, the Department of Foreign

Affairs and Trade. 'Dr Harris?' he said. 'We'd like you to go to Thailand, and I'm here to facilitate that.'

Wow, that was easy!

The man on the phone said that AUSMAT – the Australian Medical Assistance Team – would be part of an official mission authorised by DFAT. (Yes, everything's an acronym in Canberra.) AUSMAT members provide medical aid after major disasters. If there's an earthquake somewhere like Papua New Guinea, a team of doctors, nurses and logistics people will be airlifted in to help.

I had taken the AUSMAT training courses and was already on the books as an AUSMAT doctor, though I had never actually been deployed on a mission. But they knew of me, and apparently that made things easier.

'The simplest way to do this is to send you over as an AUSMAT representative, a team of one,' I was told.

Team of one? How about a team of two?

'This is important,' I said to the man from Canberra. 'I need this bloke called Craig Challen to come with me. He's my dive buddy.'

Silence.

'Um,' the man said with a sigh. 'That could be an issue.'

'If I'm going to do this,' I insisted, 'I need a trusted ally in the water with me – and more importantly, someone to help me think things through. He's a highly experienced diver. I need Craig there.'

It was then patiently explained to me that Dr Challen was not a member of AUSMAT. 'I'm sorry,' the man said.

'Let me put it another way,' I said. 'If he doesn't go, I don't go.'

I wasn't bluffing. I couldn't imagine a mission much more complex than this one. I needed my trusted friend at my side. We had a lot to thrash out here, and two heads were definitely better than one. We had to make sure we weren't doing anything dumb, or someone could die. I knew Craig would always have my back if I had to give all my attention to those kids. He wouldn't crumble under pressure, no matter how disastrous the outcome.

'Let's see what we can do.' And that was the strongest encouragement I got.

'Is he going to die, or sue us?' I was asked. 'No.'

'He might have to indemnify us, just in case.' 'Okay.'

In the end, that was pretty much it. Both of us were good to go.

On my way

Everything I'd packed for a week on the Nullarbor Plain had to come out of the truck. I decided I would bring only my wetsuit, mask, regulators and a few other bits and pieces to Thailand. Rick had told me that the front of the cave looked like a dive-shop warehouse, air tanks stacked high against the walls.

I didn't really have to tell anyone at work I was on my way. For days, people had been saying: 'Oh, I thought you'd be in Thailand by now.'

I don't want you to go

At home in Gnangara outside Perth, Craig had been discussing all of this with Heather. Not surprisingly, she had some feelings on the subject.

'I don't want you to go,' she said.

Heather had been gripped by the TV coverage of the boys in the cave. She has two grown boys of her own, and she could empathise deeply with the mums. But she was worried. 'It's wonderful they found the boys, but I don't like the way any of the rest of it sounds.'

Craig and Heather are both independent, strong-willed people. Neither one of them hesitates to speak up.

'It'll be chaos there,' Heather said. 'I know you. You'll be frustrated or reckless. Neither one of those is good.'

Craig listened. Then he said, 'Of course I'm going. What are you talking about?'

Heather didn't give up. 'Craig,' she said, 'People die. And this time the world will be watching. Have you thought of that?'

Craig heard Heather out. 'Can you take me to the airport, please?'

Heather said, sure, she'd drive him to the airport in Perth.

Dad

Before I finished packing, I called my dad. Just three weeks earlier he'd moved into a nursing home. Two and a half years earlier he'd been diagnosed with a rare oesophageal cancer – a nasty, aggressive one. The oncologist had said grimly: 'Well, Jim, if you don't have any treatment, I reckon it will be about six months. If you have chemotherapy and some radiotherapy, it might be about a year.'

Hmm . . .

He talked it over with the family and then said to the doctor, 'What about a little bit of focused radiotherapy?

A couple of zaps to delay any swallowing problems.'

Well, blow me down, it pretty much cured him!

And he had no other serious symptoms. My father had already lived four decades longer than his father and uncle. Out of the blue, he was handed the precious gift of more time!

But in early May, he had a serious fall. By then, he was having short-term memory problems. He needed closer care around the clock.

There was a new building at the nursing home where my mother had lived, and the new facility looked really nice. Reluctantly, Dad agreed to give the place a try. We drove him over and helped to move him in.

To our surprise, he didn't seem to mind it. He quickly got to know some of the other residents. He bonded instantly with the staff. People thought he was warm and funny and immensely likable – surprisingly down to earth for someone who'd been a prominent local surgeon. I could have told them that.

I'd visited him the day before, but I called him as I was packing for Thailand. 'Hi, Dad,' I said when he answered. 'How are you today?'

For the next few minutes we talked about day-to-day stuff. Then I asked if he knew about the boys trapped in a cave in Thailand.

'Of course I do,' he answered quickly.

'I'm going to go on a bit of an adventure,' I told him. 'I've been invited to help those kids.'

He answered right away, 'Good on you. Well done, Bert.'

I smiled. Dad always worried about my cave diving, but he was also very proud of me. We had a bit of a comedy routine we'd perform for each other before and after any diving trip.

'Maybe it's time to give it up,' Dad said. 'Why don't you give up the cave diving?'

'You know what, Dad? I think you're right. I'm going to give it away,' I responded, just as I had a hundred times before.

I couldn't see his eyes light up, but I could hear it in his voice. 'Oh, that's great,' he said, before delivering the punchline. 'Hang on. Hang on. You're not telling me the truth, are you?'

'Uh, maybe not, Dad.'

Dad roared with laughter. He was so happy for me.

Dr Fiona's diagnosis

I had four other people with strong opinions – Fiona and our three children: James, twenty-two; Charlie, twenty; and our daughter, Millie, who had just turned eighteen. The kids thought it would be cool for their dad to play a part in saving the boys stuck in the cave. That said, all three of them had busy lives of their own, and they weren't exactly focused on their father's cave-diving adventures. James, a talented musician, was touring with his hardcore band, Reactions. Charlie was into his downhill skateboarding. Millie had just finished high school and was in America, working at a YMCA camp in Connecticut and planning to study fashion marketing at university. But Fiona was the one who had the most say.

I had a good idea what she thought. She's my wife. She's also a doctor. Her reaction was informed by both of those facts.

She seemed especially focused on Rick's suggestion to dive the boys out unconscious and that I could play a key role in that. 'Essentially,' she said in her calm but direct way, 'you're the doctor there. These boys are your patients. You're the anaesthetist. But there will be no light or backup inside the cave. It's critical-care medicine. Just do as you always do.'

Fiona wasn't worried about me dying in the cave. She understood, far more clearly than I did, what the real risk was.

I had told her about Rick's warning, that we'd better prepare ourselves for the worst imaginable news.

She put the question directly: 'So what impact will this have on you – emotionally, professionally, personally – if even one of those boys dies? What happens then?'

It was impossible to know, of course. But I got her point.

'You may not be able to save those children. You might be blamed, completely unfairly. You might blame yourself. That's a reality you may not be able to control. What will you be feeling then? How do you go back to work knowing you killed one of those children?'

I could imagine as well as she could how future patients might respond. But Fiona put it into words: 'I don't want Dr Harris to anaesthetise me. He's the one who killed those boys in Thailand.'

7

SPECIAL K

HARRY

In the entire history of medicine, as far as I knew, only one person had ever been in the water under anaesthetic and survived. His name was Edgar Pask, and he was filmed doing it. A quiet man, Pask was a British doctor and military officer who conducted research for the Royal Air Force's Medical Services branch during World War II. I devoured his work while I was training to be an anaesthetist and he became one of my professional heroes. Pask was willing to stir up a bit of controversy if it would save lives, and he did not hesitate to put his own life on the line.

Anaesthesia and water can mix

Pask and his New Zealand–born mentor, anaesthetist Robert Reynolds Macintosh, were asked to test an airman's inflatable life-jacket design. Named after curvy early-Hollywood sex symbol Mae West, the jackets resembled a large female bosom. These Mae Wests were designed to keep an unconscious person floating face up in choppy waters, should they parachute into the English Channel under enemy fire. Quite a few Allied crewmen had been found dead, face down in the water, floating in their old-style life jackets with water in their lungs.

Pask worried that conscious volunteers might be righting themselves, so he settled on a bolder course. He would strap on one of the Mae West jackets, have himself anaesthetised with ether delivered through a tube, and then be thrown into the pool at the lab. He ordered the entire experiment be filmed, so he'd have a reliable record. Edgar Pask was a jump-in-the-deep-end kind of guy.

The experiment succeeded. Even unconscious, Pask remained face up in his new Mae West. The film of Pask's experiments was shown to Allied aircrews to boost their morale and let them know, in Pask's words, that 'something was being done'.

Several times Dr Pask sank to the bottom of the wave pool and sucked in a lot of water. When he came out of the pool, he was rushed to hospital and remained there long enough to regain his composure and his strength. Sadly, Edgar Pask died unexpectedly in 1966 at the age of fifty-three. To me he was a great inspiration and one of the unsung heroes of World War II. He'd shown that anaesthesia and water *can* mix. He might even become a hero of the Thai cave rescue.

But I wasn't confident that sedating the children was even possible two and a half kilometres into a pitch-dark, flooded cave, much less a safe way of diving them out.

What germs and bacteria were dancing around in all that cave water? Every five minutes, another objection popped into my head.

Drugs

If I had to do this, what drug would I use to sedate the boys? Lorazepam? Too long-acting. Midazolam? Too unpredictable. Clonidine? Not potent enough. Then I started thinking about a drug called ketamine.

For fifty years ketamine has proven itself a reliable sedative in the operating theatre. A shot of ketamine, either intravenously or into the muscle, will send a patient into a trancelike state while providing pain relief and hypnosis. It's a nice drug with relatively few side effects. Blood pressure, breathing and airway reflexes – they all remain pretty stable.

Ketamine quickly found a place for itself in hospitals around the world. It wasn't the subtlest or most sophisticated drug, but it was safe, predictable and easy to work with. Veterinary surgeons also started using ketamine to sedate horses and other large animals, and eventually added dogs, cats, rabbits, rats and other smaller creatures to the K-list.

I talked with Craig about this. He'd used more ketamine in his practice on animals than I ever had in mine on humans. But both of us had the same feelings about the drug. It was a reliable workhorse and relatively difficult to screw up. Amateurs might even be able to administer it.

Ketamine had other advantages, too, that might be important in a flooded cave with patients I couldn't thoroughly screen or even weigh. With ketamine, the dosage doesn't have to be all that exact, and it's more difficult to overdose a patient on ketamine than on other anaesthetics. It's fast-acting, beginning to take effect within thirty seconds of being injected into a vein. But it can also be injected into muscle.

Ketamine's major problem was that its effects don't last all that long. After half an hour or so, depending on the dosage, it's common for a patient on ketamine to rouse. There was no way one injection was going to last for the three or more hours it could take to get each of the boys out. Somewhere along the way, they'd need to be given a top-up dose. Maybe once. Maybe several times. Who would do that? How would they do it, and where? Without top-ups, the boys were sure to wake up on the way out of the cave, creating who-knows-what panic and mayhem, and putting everyone in danger, including themselves.

Phone a friend

With all this bouncing around in my head, I decided to seek an outside opinion. I contacted a good friend and colleague of mine in Adelaide, country GP James Doube. James is an inventive jack-of-all-trades, a multi-talented brainiac who can come up with a solution to almost any challenge laid in front of him. He'd spent nearly four years in the Antarctic and on Macquarie Island, a Tasmanian ecological reserve about halfway between New Zealand and Antarctica with a human population of twenty to forty people and more penguins passing through than anyone could count. He keeps going back – and not just as a doctor. He does every thing from pest eradication to helping scientists collect data on a broad class of carnivorous, fin-footed, semiaquatic marine mammals formally known as pinnipeds. You and I call them seals.

James had occasionally been asked to anaesthetise a seal, and he'd told me about one he'd put under with ketamine while he was working in the Antarctic.

'James,' I said when I got him on the phone, 'I want to run something by you. You've done a lot of weird stuff with anaesthesia in strange places.'

I told him my problem. 'What do you think about giving the kids some ketamine before diving them out?'

'Remember that story I told you about the seal who got away, the one that kept swimming even though he was totally out?' he asked.

How could I forget? The seal had escaped and jumped into the water. James was worried that it was going to drown. But no. Though it seemed to be sleeping soundly, it kept swimming around, its nose out of the water, apparently breathing comfortably.

'Even when he was underwater, he was still making sure he could breathe,' James said. 'I think your kids should be fine.'

'That's very reassuring, James,' I said sarcastically, though I did in fact take some comfort from the wacky anecdote.

'They should do at least as well as the seal,' he said.

That was the closest thing to relevant experience, good or bad, I had, even though it involved a seal and not a child. My old friend's words didn't convince me, but they did inch me towards the view that Rick's suggestion might not be totally absurd.

I had no idea if the children in Thailand would behave like South Pole pinnipeds. But my mate James seemed to think they would.

8

FLYING HIGH

HARRY

My Qantas flight to Melbourne's Tullamarine Airport left Adelaide on Thursday evening. I was to meet up with Craig there for our overnight flight to Bangkok.

As Thai Airways TG 462 started boarding, Craig's plane still hadn't arrived from Perth. As I settled into my roomy business-class aisle seat, there was still no Craig. He ended up missing the flight by ten minutes, so there'd be no midair strategising. But it turned out I had a fellow rescuer aboard.

'You know,' a helpful attendant told me as soon as the cabin door was closed, 'there's another Australian diver on the plane.'

She pointed out a very fit-looking young man, two rows behind me.

A few minutes after take-off, I wandered back and introduced myself. He said his name was Mark Usback. 'I'm with the AFP SRG,' he said softly. 'I'll be supervising our divers.'

I knew what AFP was – the Australian Federal Police – but what did SRG mean? I found out later it was Specialist Response Group. Mark was impressive and seemingly capable, a friendly bloke, but I got the distinct impression that friendly wasn't the only way he was trained to confront the world.

After we'd chatted and I'd returned to my seat, the attendant offered a glass of champagne.

'Well, thank you very much,' I said as I set the glass on my armrest. I began reading my deployment orders, taking the occasional sip of my champagne. There was a huge amount of bureaucratic waffle required to get two blokes from Australia to help rescue some kids. All the jargon quickly made my head hurt. I accepted the attendant's offer of a refill.

Yes, business class is nicer than economy.

As I was getting comfortable, I couldn't help but notice that AFP SRG Mark was sipping on sparkling water instead of champagne. And he seemed to do a double take when he looked at me. But we had a long flight ahead of us. So when the attendant offered me another refill, I naturally said yes.

It was then I came across the first reference to the Australian government's code of conduct.

Uh-oh! Why hadn't anyone mentioned that?

I read: 'This is a dry mission. Consumption of alcohol is strictly prohibited.'

Now Mark's glances made a lot more sense to me.

After I arrived in Bangkok, a young Thai man came over and introduced himself. He was Kittanu Supasamsen – 'Nu for short,' he said in perfect, polite English. He was a liaison officer and interpreter working in Thailand for the Australian government. He too was heading to Chiang Rai and then on to Mae Sai for the cave rescue. His job usually involved getting rowdy Australians out of jail and quickly out of Thailand, so the cave rescue was a new adventure for him. I told him that Craig and I would try not to behave like typical Aussies on a Thai holiday.

Then Kittanu told me that something had gone tragically wrong deep inside the cave early that Friday morning. Saman Gunan, a former Thai Navy SEAL, had drowned; he was only 37 years old. Kittanu didn't know exactly what had happened. But he recognised, as I did, that this was an ominous milestone in the rescue campaign.

'The first fatality at the cave,' he said. 'We can only hope it's the last one.'

Bangkok to Chiang Rai

Once we landed in Bangkok, I boarded a shuttle bus to the domestic terminal, where I would pick up my ninety-minute, early-morning Bangkok Airways flight to the regional capital of Chiang Rai.

'Are you rescuing the boys or covering the rescue?' a young woman on the bus asked, without even introducing herself.

She couldn't have seen what was written on the back of my light-blue button-down shirt: Australian doctor. Or maybe she had, and that's why I'd caught her eye. We were both heading to a place that isn't a huge tourist destination.

'We're *hoping* we can help rescue them,' I said. After Rick's chilling warning, I'd promised myself: no over-confidence. No false optimism.

The young woman must have picked up on my tone. 'You never know,' she said cheerily. 'It could happen.'

I had left in such a rush, I had no visa and little idea about where I'd be staying or for how long. I just hoped some immigration officer would take pity on me. The Qantas agents in Adelaide had looked the other way when I dumped my massively heavy load of excess baggage at the check-in counter – though one of them did sniff sarcastically: 'How many divers do they need over there?' She must have just checked in Mark Usback and all his gear.

When our Chang Rai flight was finally ready to board, Kittanu Supasamsen and I walked across the tarmac and climbed the aluminium steps to the plane. As we both found our seats – there was no business class this time – I noticed that the young woman from the shuttle bus was a couple of rows in front of me. A few minutes after take-off, she turned to talk to me.

'Have you helped rescue people from a cave before?' she asked.

'Not live ones,' I said.

After we'd landed she tried to draw me out again.

'Don't you think it might be better just to wait out the rain and send in supplies?'

'I think it's better to try,' I said.

She sounded sceptical. 'Men are really going to dive those boys out?' she asked.

'That's the plan,' I said.

When I asked what brought her to Chiang Rai, she said matter-of-factly that she was a journalist working on an article about the rescue for a Canadian magazine.

A journalist? I clammed up in a hurry after that. I was pretty sure I wasn't supposed to be talking to journalists.

Farewell Saman Gunan

I stepped off the plane and onto the aerobridge at Chiang Rai's international airport. A light rain was falling on the tarmac. Any rain was bad until we got those children out of the cave. Others were staring out of the windows too.

What are they looking at? I wondered.

It was a ramp ceremony for the dead Navy SEAL. What else could be so solemn and so grand, with a Buddhist monk in saffron robes and a Thai military guard of honour?

Finally, the honour guard carried the flag-draped casket towards a Royal Thai Navy plane.

I still didn't know many details about what had happened to the former SEAL. But I saw now what was at stake in this mission. Not just the lives of a dozen children and their young assistant coach, but the lives of all who were coming together to rescue them, including mine and Craig's.

Stick like glue

As I wheeled my heavy load of gear out of baggage claim, Kittanu and I were met by two earnest young Australians named Michael Costa and Cameron Lindsay. They were on short-term deployment with DFAT's crisis-response team. We soon discovered that they would stick like glue to Craig and me.

Once the gear was loaded and we'd all climbed into the DFAT van, I announced to Michael, Cameron and Kittanu: 'Okay, take me to the cave.'

Not until certain steps were taken first, I was told. The most pressing was my authority to practise medicine in Thailand. I was an accredited specialist anaesthetist in Australia, of course, but that carried little weight in Thailand. The DFAT guys had filled out the paperwork on my behalf, but now it was up to the Thais.

'Until we hear something,' Michael cautioned, 'you need to remain in the hotel.'

Oh, great! I thought. The skies might open at any moment and drown everyone, and where would I be? Stuck in my room.

The van took us through bumper-to-bumper traffic to the Wang Thong hotel (air conditioning, bar fridge, free wi-fi), which was just outside Mae Sai's teeming market and a two-minute walk from Thailand's busy border with Myanmar. I checked into the hotel around four, unpacked my luggage and my diving gear and then waited. Around seven-thirty, as it was getting dark, he finally called me.

'We have it,' he said. 'You've been approved.' Craig would be coming soon, Michael assured me, but I didn't want to wait. I left my gear in the room and climbed into the van with my minders for the fifteen-minute drive to the cave.

'Craig can meet us up there,' I said.

The cave

The van turned right off the two-lane highway and onto the bumpy road to the entrance of the cave, but I hardly noticed the landscape. The air was close and muggy, and I kept glancing up at the heavy clouds hanging above. There was no telling when they might open up with another burst of monsoon rains.

As we got closer, cars and TV-satellite trucks were everywhere. It looked like we were driving up to a music festival or the AFL grand final. People were walking in groups along the small road. There were vendors selling plastic bottles of water, and people in army fatigues, soccer jerseys, simple dresses and diving gear. There were women standing over pots of hot food. There were boys kicking a soccer ball – boys about the same age as the ones trapped in the cave. And media people. Everywhere.

I climbed out of the van and stepped straight into a sea of reporters, producers, presenters and what must have been a dozen TV cameras, all pointing at me. 'How are the boys?'

'What condition are they in?'

'How much longer can they survive in there?'

'Are you going into the cave?'

'What's the best option at this point?'

'How long do you expect the rain to hold off?'

They had been at the scene for days, and I had just arrived. What was I supposed to say?

'Michael,' I muttered under my breath, 'just take me straight to where the British divers are. I want to talk to them.'

That's all it took. Michael led me to a squat concrete-block building, that had, until recently, been a rangers' office for the Tham Luang – Khun Nam Nang Non Forest Park. Now, it was headquarters for the growing contingent of British divers. Open glass louvres. Concrete floor. Fluorescent lighting. Mismatched plastic chairs. Dirty caving gear piled haphazardly on the floor, and a dank pervasive aroma. What it lacked in style and comfort, it more than made up for in proximity, just up the hill from the muddy entrance to the cave.

'Hey, mate!'

Rick Stanton greeted me like the old friends we were. He couldn't have been more welcoming. At Rick's side was John Volanthen, or JV as Rick calls him. An IT guy who grew up in Brighton in the UK, John is an ultramarathon runner with a dry sense of humour and excellent technical skills. He's been diving since he was a scrawny Scout. He and Rick have set records for the longest distance into a cave, and the deepest dive in a British cave; they've taken part in cave rescues and body recoveries. John is one of the legends. We'd exchanged emails, but we'd never actually met till then.

'You heard about the Navy SEAL?' Rick asked me. I nodded.

He said he and John had met Saman Gunan soon after they'd arrived at the cave. 'He was a lot like so many of these volunteers,' Rick said. 'Just a tremendous amount of heart, ready to jump in and help, even at risk to themselves. His death makes everything seem more real to the rest of us.'

With Michael from DFAT in tow, John gave me a quick tour of the area, trying to steer clear of the media. They showed me where the Australian Federal Police tent was, and I ducked inside. That's where I was, introducing myself to the AFP divers, when Craig appeared.

'Oh, you finally made it,' he said with a grin.

'And g'day to you too,' I said.

Craig had come straight from the airport. No hotel arrest for him. It was almost 9 p.m. by then and all his gear was still in the van.

'What have I missed?' Craig asked. He doesn't like missing things.

'Nothing, mate,' I answered. 'Just getting started.'

9

DEAR MUM

HARRY

Soon after Craig and I arrived in the British bunker, Chris Jewell and Jason Mallinson came staggering in, just back from a food-delivery run. Their wetsuits were dripping, and they were carrying their cylinders, fins and masks, looking thoroughly knackered from the long dive and the short hike up the hill.

Chris and Jason were two of the most experienced and highly skilled members of Britain's long-running Cave Diving Group underwater explorers who'd dived with Rick and John for years. Chris, a 35-year-old computer-software consultant from Cheddar, Somerset, was an avid caver before he turned to cave diving in 2006 and started organising diving expeditions into deep, vertical caves. Jason, an amazingly fit 50-year-old dad of a toddler, was a dour Yorkshireman from Huddersfield whose day job involved hanging off the sides of large structures and required many of the same skills needed in climbing and caving.

Food at last

'We got some rations from the US Air Force guys, a bunch of high-protein, high-sugar, high-energy stuff,' Chris said.

'The kids were very happy to see us,' Jason added. 'Better make that *happy to see the food*.'

The boys had been eating far more than anyone had expected. 'We thought we had them supplied for one to two weeks,' Rick said. 'They went through that food in four days. There's been a bit of diarrhoea and some upset stomachs, but nothing too severe – not yet, anyway. They're just hungry, I guess.'

All this was important. The kids had been without solid food for the first ten days. They needed food for energy. Their growing bodies craved nutrition. I wasn't an expert, but I knew they were at risk of something called *refeeding syndrome*. Starving people who are fed too much too soon can suffer dizziness, seizures, coma and even heart failure. The boys had been fed now, but we'd need to watch them carefully. Refeeding syndrome can be fatal, and the signs may not appear for a few days. However long it took to get them out of there, it was crucial the kids remain as healthy as possible. Rescuing them would be far more difficult and far more dangerous if they started falling ill.

The biggest news that day, though, was that Chris and Jason had notes from the boys and Coach Ekk to pass on to their families. One of the Thai Navy SEALs had given him a pen and a pad of wet-notes – a special kind of waterproof paper – so he could make notes about the state of the kids' health. While they were in the cave, he'd thought, *It might be good to have them write something to their parents.* So he said, 'Here you go. Half a page for each of you. Write a message to your mum or dad or whoever you want to, anything you want to say. Just put it on the pad. We'll take it out with us and give it to them.'

Letters from the cave

Each of the boys got busy scribbling away on the specially treated paper, trying to ease their parents' concerns in two or three well-chosen lines.

Mum and Dad, I love you, please don't worry. I am safe now. Love you all. – Pong

Mum and Dad, don't worry about me, please, I am fine. Please tell Pee Yod, get ready to take me to eat fried chicken. – Titan

Mum and Dad, I love you, and I love Nong too. If I can get out, please take me to eat crispy pork. Love you Mum, Dad, Nong. – Nick

The boys all signed with their nicknames. Each of them had one, as many Thais do. The sentiments they expressed were so childlike, so simple, so pure, it was possible to read their words and to feel you knew them, at least a little. These little notes were our first real introduction to the boys as individuals. Their story was so gripping, so human, so easy to relate to – and yet no one outside of Mae Sai really knew these boys as anything beyond 'the boys'.

These little notes provided an early glimpse, and everyone devoured them.

Please don't worry, Mum and Dad. I have been gone for two weeks. I will come back and help you with the shop when I can. I will try to come soon. – Biw

I love you, Mum and Dad, please don't worry about me. I love you all. – Night

Mum, are you well at home? I am fine. Please tell my teacher as well. Love you, Mum Nam Hom. – Mark

Mum, Dad, Brother and Sister and family, please don't worry, I am very happy. – Tee

I am fine, it is a bit cold, but don't worry. Please don't forget my birthday. – Dom

No need to worry about us any more. I miss you all. I really want to go out so much. – Adul

Don't worry. I miss you all, Grandpa, Aunty, Dad, Mum and Nong. I love you all. I am happy, the SEAL team is taking care of us very well. Love you all. – Mick

I love you, Mum and Dad, please don't worry. I can take care of myself. – Tern

I am safe, please don't worry. I love you, Mum, Dad and everyone. – Note

Coach Ekk wrote two notes, the first to his aunt and grandmother:

Dear Aunty and Grandmother, I am fine, please don't worry about me too much. Please take care of your health. Please tell Grandmother to make crispy pork skin with dipping *sauce for me. I will come and eat it when I get out. Love you all.*

In his second note, Coach Ekk reflected on just how deeply he took his responsibility for the boys:

Dear parents, we are all fine. The team is taking care of us very well. I promise that I will take the best care of the boys. Thanks for all your support and I apologise to all the parents.

Who could read a note like that and not feel torn for this obviously caring young man?

As happy as the notes would certainly make the families, there was a darker possibility here, as well. As everyone knew, we were only one rainstorm away from true catastrophe. Given the boys' uncertain futures, these short, hastily scribbled messages truly might be the families' final connection with their lost sons.

It was hard not to think about all these possibilities as Jason and Chris relaxed with their mates back in the British bunker while the SEALs, the coach and the children remained behind in the cave. It was a huge responsibility for all concerned.

I was happy for the families who'd finally had some contact with the children they hadn't seen for two weeks now. Of course the boys needed food and water, and writing notes to their families would keep their spirits up, but the most important thing was getting them out of there as soon as possible. It was nearly midnight when I sat down next to Rick. 'Okay,' I said, 'can we talk this through? Where are we up to? What's the plan?'

What next?

The concrete bunker wasn't much of a conference room, but we pulled some plastic chairs into a circle and got right to it. Besides Craig and me, there were Rick and John, Chris and Jason, plus Derek Anderson and Charles Hodges from the US Air Force Pararescue service – the PJs they called themselves, for parajumpers. The Americans had rushed to the scene and quickly proven themselves expert coordinators and organisers, providing much-needed order amid the chaos outside the cave. They were natural leaders. At one point, British cavers Gary Mitchell and Vern Unsworth popped in. Michael Costa, our DFAT minder, was in the room with his notebook, scribbling down everything that was said.

Rick spoke first. 'Okay,' he said. 'A quick update on where things stand.'

He breezed through all the stuff we already knew. That after the divers had spent several days laying guide rope and searching for signs of life, he and John had located the boys on Monday. That they were stranded on a muddy shelf, just past a stretch of the cave known as Pattaya Beach, which was usually dry but had flooded after the rains. That all the boys were alive and seemed fairly healthy, mentally and physically. That a four-man Thai Navy SEAL team, including a doctor, had been looking after them since Tuesday. That food and other supplies were being ferried in. 'We're stocking up the larder as full as we can,' Rick said, 'not knowing how much longer they're going to be there. And of course, everyone is hoping it won't rain again. 'Anyway,' he continued, 'we've been putting together a plan, a detailed recipe for how we think we can get the kids out. I believe you guys know about some of this,' he said, looking at Craig and me. 'Some of it maybe not. If you're ready, we can run you through it now.'

'Eager to hear it,' Craig said.

The plan

Rick jumped right in. 'The plan revolves around you getting to the kids and sedating them for the dive out,' he said. 'If you can do that, our guys will dive them out.'

'Before they regain consciousness,' John added.

'*Before*,' Rick agreed.

Rick's plan was to outfit each of the boys in full diving gear. Air tank. Full-face mask. Wetsuit. A harness and buoyancy-compensation device to keep them floating horizontally. The divers had clearly worked through many of the details already.

'Positive-pressure full face masks,' Rick said, 'so they can breathe as normally as possible. And front-mounted cylinders.'

'Okay,' I said tentatively.

He moved on to the next part of the plan. 'Two divers per kid,' he said. 'One in front. One behind. We figure the trip should take a couple of hours. We'll dive them out as quickly as we can. We can probably do six of them the first day. Bang, bang, bang, one after another, moving swiftly through the cave. We don't want anyone waking up before we get them out of there.'

'Wait a second,' I said. 'Two divers per kid?' To me, it sounded like a traffic jam.

Harry's view

'We haven't seen the cave ourselves,' I began, 'so I can't be sure whether this is right or wrong. But it sounds like a very dangerous way to do it. There are all these choke points and restrictions in there, right? What happens when one of the kids starts to wake up or panic or flail around? You're going to stop and try to fix the problem. You have a diver in the front, a diver behind. You're in zero visibility. You're not going to be able to see each other. You won't be able to communicate. And then the next bunch of guys are going to bump into you from behind, and then the next bunch of guys are going to bump into them. Before you know it, I can see three dead kids and some dead divers. No one will have any idea what's happening. No one will know what to do. Communication will be impossible. It just sounds like a very dangerous, overly complex way to do it – a potential disaster, as I see it.'

Well, that was met with quiet stares.

It's always dicey raising objections to someone else's plan. Craig and I had just arrived in Thailand. We were the new guys at the cave. Rick and his team had been there for days, working diligently, making progress, winning converts, proving themselves. They knew the cave. They had found the children. And oh, by the way – they were also the most talented and highly respected cave divers in the world. Now Craig and I were coming in and criticising their carefully crafted plan. But if we were going to be involved in the rescue, especially if we were being asked to do something so dangerous and completely unprecedented, I couldn't sit there quietly, nodding dumbly. I would have understood if there had been some pushback against my criticisms. But that wasn't how they reacted at all.

Rick was still gazing at me intently, but he didn't seem resentful. I knew he was considering the points I'd made. He wasn't agreeing. He wasn't disagreeing. He just nodded deliberately, as if to say, *Go on.*

So I did.

'I'd like you to consider the possibility of one diver and one child,' I said. 'And a good amount of separation between them. I wouldn't try to do too many in a single day.'

'One diver?' Jason interrupted. He sounded sceptical.

'One diver is better than two,' I said.

That was a lesson Craig and I had learned the hard way seven years earlier, diving the body of our good friend Agnes out of Tank Cave, when I ended up in an alcove with Craig behind me pushing forwards. It was a frightening lesson we'd never forget. That dive was much shorter than this one would be. And sadly, of course, we didn't have to worry about Agnes's breathing, or whether water was seeping into her mask.

'You're trying to do something complicated,' I said. 'But you can't communicate when something starts to go wrong. You can't even see each other well enough to use hand signals. You can't say, "Stop and wait while I fix this." You can't tell if the guy in front of you is all right, and he can't tell if you're all right.'

All of that had been a challenge for Craig and me with Agnes. The problems would be multiplied here.

'Say you're at the back,' I said. 'You'll feel the child thrashing around. You can tell something's going wrong.

But you can't see or feel exactly what the problem is. Is it that we can't get through the opening in front of us? Is it that you're worried about the kid and you've turned around? Have you lost the line? Are we now off the line, and I'm the bloke who's supposed to be navigating? Are we lost now? Any number of things could be going wrong. If you can't even see each other to work out how to solve that problem right away, things are going to disintegrate. You're a metre out of my reach, no more than the length of a child's body, but we might as well be a mile apart from each other. I've got a kid who's starting to wake up or might be panicking. I don't know if you're there or not. It could be anything. Everything can go pear-shaped really, really fast.

'It all gets easier,' I said, 'when it's one on one. If it's just me and the kid, I know that I'm the one who has to keep hold of that line or I'm in trouble. I'm not taking my mind off anything – not even for a second. If the kid starts to have a problem, I can lock the line under my arm and try to sort it out. If I come to a pinch point that requires a bit of feeling around to work out exactly how to get through, I can take as long as I need to without worrying about the guy behind me, who will be worrying about what's happening. And in the worst-case scenario . . .' – I hated to even raise the possibility, but how could I not? – 'if the kid drowns, I'll deal with that and keep moving forwards. Once you're in the water with the boy, that's what you're going to have to do. There will be no turning back.'

A solo act

I knew I had given quite a speech there, but this was no time to put a sock in it. I didn't think what I was proposing would seem all that radical, not to world-class cave divers. Much of cave diving is done solo, a far safer way of doing things when the cave is tight, the visibility is bad and you're not sure what you are going to find. Even when you step into the water with a partner, that doesn't mean you'll swim right beside each other throughout the entire dive. Underwater in a cave, a little distance can actually be your friend. Cave diving might be a team sport, but it's fundamentally a solo act. You can watch each other's backs. You can help in an emergency. But if you're not worrying about a second diver right there next to you, you can slow down and do everything at your own speed. It's easier to focus. It's a lot less complex. When everything is simplified it's much safer.

And apparently, Rick didn't disagree. 'Okay,' he finally said. 'I see what you mean.' I understood that Craig and I weren't there for our diving prowess. Rick and his guys were unmatchable. We were there primarily because of our medical expertise. But our insights were a bonus, I suppose, and the Brits were still willing to listen to us.

There was some discussion of my one-diver-one-boy proposal, but soon everyone was saying, 'Okay, that sounds all right.'

Not bad for our initial meeting.

Now all we had to organise was everything else.

10
QUESTION EVERYTHING
HARRY

The British didn't get to decide. Nor did the Americans. Nor did Craig and I. Coach Ekk and the boys definitely didn't get to decide. Any rescue plan would need the explicit approval and support of the Thai government, the Thai medical authorities, the Thai foreign ministry, the Thai first responders, and most of all, it seemed, the Thai military. We weren't in charge. They were.

Craig and I had both been to Thailand several times before. It is a beautiful country with an ancient culture and some of the gentlest and most welcoming people on earth. From the 24-hour mega-capital of Bangkok to the world-class beach resorts of Phuket to the temples and shrines of the north, Thailand is an intensely spiritual and thoroughly global country where the traditional and the modern live side by side every day.

Who's running the show?

The Kingdom of Thailand, as the nation is officially called, is a constitutional monarchy, and although the revolution of 1932 stripped the monarchy of power, it was not abolished, and members of the royal family are still revered in Thailand. Since that time, there have been some periods of democracy, but real power is usually wielded by the military.

As the Tham Luang drama began, Thailand was again ruled by the military, calling themselves the National Council for Peace and Order. The Thai military authorities at first were confident that their people could handle everything. But the generals quickly came to recognise, especially after Saman Gunan died, that a flooded cave was a uniquely perilous environment that Thai personnel didn't have the training to handle alone. This was a job that called for high-level international expertise and cooperation, though the Thais would never give up ultimate control.

In navigating all this, we did have one secret weapon: Josh Morris.

An American from Utah who ran a caving and climbing business in Thailand, Josh was married to a well-connected Thai woman and spoke fluent Thai. He explained to the Thai generals how the international cave divers could be helpful and explained Thai customs and etiquette to the divers. 'There's a Thai word that means "connector",' he said to us. '*Cheụ̀xm*. It's the same word you use for welding. You need a connector here.'

And with Josh we had one.

Chiang Rai governor Narongsak Osottanakorn had been put in charge of the overall rescue at an operational level. Though his job as governor of the northern province had recently ended, he remained on duty. Numerous top Thai officials, including Prime Minister Prayut Chan-o-cha, a former general, were involved in many of the major decisions. Certainly they had to sign off on any rescue plan.

At our first meeting in the British bunker, sedation had definitely been the favourite plan, but we hadn't decided on anything yet. Whatever we settled on would need the blessing of the military leaders.

Craig's view

Craig remained a leading sceptic. He wasn't at all convinced that sedation would be necessary. It was still worth exploring, he said, whether the boys could be outfitted in wetsuits and full underwater-breathing gear and dived out of the cave the normal way, each escorted by an experienced diver.

'These kids are tough,' Craig argued. 'Look at how well they've done in the cave so far.'

He had a point. According to the Brits, the boys had been unbelievably resilient, maintaining their health, their sanity and their good spirits for two severely challenging weeks. Their team spirit, the guidance of Coach Ekk, whatever it was – under impossible circumstances, they had held up remarkably well.

'Maybe we should just give it a go,' Craig suggested. 'See how they do in the water. Take them out for a dive. Who knows? They might surprise us all.'

That was pure Craig, putting his faith in people. He knew that motivated people, including children, could accomplish amazing things. But the consequences of failure would be severe. No one else seemed eager to test-drive Craig's let's-just-try-it approach. Even he didn't push the idea too hard. With divers as young and as thoroughly inexperienced as these, he conceded, panic is awfully hard to hold back. A couple of unexpected gulps of water really could change everything.

'They'll be experiencing something they've never experienced before,' Craig admitted. 'It will seem very threatening.'

We hadn't been in the cave yet, but we both knew what to expect. The jutting rocks. The low ceilings. The constricted corners. The narrow openings. We were used to these conditions and would be completely comfortable, but not so the boys.

'Whether they're conscious or not, they'll be banging against rock as they move through the cave. It's inevitable,' Craig said. 'And being unable to see can be pretty disorienting.'

Though the knocks and scrapes wouldn't be life-threatening, they might be painful, and startling enough to shatter a newbie's confidence. Could youthful exuberance or Buddhist calm really stand up to that?

'You can imagine someone coping with it for a short while,' Craig said finally. 'But for hours? That's unrealistic, I suppose.'

Craig ended up at the same place as the rest of us. Full sedation, anaesthesia in fact. Positive-pressure face masks. Hands and feet bound. One diver, one boy. Thirteen neat little packages gliding underwater through the cave.

Drugs

I had a couple of small but important suggestions still to add. One thing we should do, I said, was give each of the boys an anti-anxiety medication before the dive, something like alprazolam. It wouldn't knock out the pre-trip jitters entirely, but it would take the edge off them. I'd also give each of them a shot of atropine, which would dry out their mouths, to prevent them choking on their saliva.

Everyone seemed to think both those suggestions were sensible.

Step by step, we were getting closer to a working plan. Now, all we had to do was pull it apart, tweak it, test it and sell it to the Thais.

So was there a middle ground here? That was one question. They kept coming as the night wore on.

Would light sedation be enough? If so, the boys might still be able to follow simple instructions in the water, control their own breathing and be more attuned to what was happening around them.

Turn right. Go slow here. Okay, walk across this sandy stretch.

With a little practice, couldn't we teach a slightly medicated boy how to wiggle through a narrow constriction, or to blow water out of his leaky mask?

But the instant that something went wrong – and we all knew that *something* would go wrong – would that mild sedation be enough to stop a child panicking? No, it probably wouldn't, everyone agreed, not if he thought he was about to drown.

Panic

Rick reminded us then of what had happened with the four Thai water workers trapped in chamber 3. 'They were absolutely terrified when we tried to dive them out,' he said. 'They were certain they were going to die.'

To escape, the men had to dive through the short sump connecting chambers 3 and 2. It was only ten metres, but the men had no previous scuba experience and Rick and John had to ram them through a half-hour beginner's diving course. It hadn't done much good. The men were too scared to stay and too scared to go. When they'd finally agreed to press ahead, at least two of the Thai water workers had panicked severely, so much so that Rick and John both thought someone might die.

'These were grown men, not children, experienced adults all of them,' John said. 'And they were in chamber three, close to the entrance of the cave. The dive was only about twenty or thirty seconds. Yet they were convinced they wouldn't make it out alive.'

Once they'd stepped out of the cave, all four of the Thai water workers disappeared into the darkness, and neither Rick nor John had seen them since. If this was how four adults reacted, how would a dozen children and their young coach respond?

Hearing that story seemed to strike a chord with most of the people in the room. I'm sure many of us remembered our first cave dives, how strange, difficult or exhilarating they had been.

'The reality can't be ignored,' Rick said. 'As long as those children are awake and alert, there's no way they are coming out of that cave without being terrified.'

Under these circumstances, terror meant panic, and panic could be fatal – for the children and even for the rescuers who had come all this way to save them.

After we'd talked things over a while longer, Rick moved in to close the deal. 'So, Harry,' he asked, 'can you do this or not?'

Can you?

Time was ticking by, and Rick wanted an answer – *soon.* I was inching closer to one, thoroughly convinced we had to do something without delay. The monsoon rains could roar in at any minute, making all this rescue talk irrelevant. As for the other ideas that were still kicking around, none of them held much promise any more. The drillers and the drainers had already tried and failed. Somehow or other, cave divers would have to go in there and haul those boys out.

I was getting more comfortable with the idea of anaesthesia, too. I'd been highly sceptical when Rick first ran that idea past me in Adelaide, but I had reluctantly come most of the way around. On a long list of terrible options, it really was the best we had. I felt sure that ketamine was the most appropriate drug. I felt good about the one-diver-one-boy strategy. I felt good about the skill and professionalism of the divers on Rick's team. We had the best anywhere.

So what was the problem? Who or what was I doubting?

'I can't agree to anything,' I said to Rick and the others, 'until I dive the cave. I need to feel confident I can do it, that I can physically do it. That I'll be in the condition I need to be to do my job. I have to see the place where I'm going to sedate these boys. And I want to meet them. I *need* to meet them.'

Meeting the boys

'You need to *meet* them?' Jason asked, as if he hadn't quite heard me.

'They'll be my patients,' I said. 'I need to meet them.'

Some of my concerns were medical. Some were psychological. Some were physical.

The truth was I had doubts about my own physical fitness and my ability to operate in the cave. I was pathetically out of shape. I'd put on some extra kilos. I had been ignoring the nagging pleas of Fiona and my children to get to the gym. I hadn't done much diving lately, and it showed.

'Just look at me,' I said. 'I haven't done a big dive like this for a while. I just need to dive the cave and make sure I can handle everything.'

It was important to see exactly where the boys were. Other people had described it to me: the boys and their coach were all crowded together on a ledge up a muddy slope from flooded Pattaya Beach. I could point to it on the map of the cave Vern had supplied. I could more or less picture it in my head. But none of that was a substitute for diving there and seeing it with my own eyes.

Somewhere on the ledge or down below it, I was going to have to set up a makeshift operating theatre where I could anaesthetise each of the boys and prepare them for their unconscious dive out. It would be dark in there. The conditions would be far from sanitary. I wasn't sure if I would have a stable, level place to do the injections. How would I hold the boys and stop them falling into the water prematurely after they were asleep? Was there something I could sit on? Was there a dry spot near the water – dry enough to perform my injections but close enough to the water that the dive could begin right away?

Was there a place where we could lay the boy down while his hands and feet were bound together and other last-minute preparations were made? It was impossible to answer any of these questions without going there.

'You guys have all been in the cave and seen the kids,' I said. 'I think Craig and I should dive the cave tomorrow.'

Swimming-pool dress rehearsal

I got pushback on that, especially from Jason. It turned out that the British divers had other plans for Saturday – important plans – and wanted Craig and me to come along. They had arranged a rehearsal dive in an indoor swimming pool at a school in Mae Sai about a twenty-minute drive from the cave. As closely as possible, they wanted to duplicate the conditions of the rescue, right down to recruiting three teenagers from a local swimming club to play the roles of the sedated Wild Boars – a small boy, a medium-size boy and a larger one. The Thai Navy SEALs were sending people to watch the rehearsal. So was the US military. Two local paramedic crews had agreed to come with their ambulances, just in case anything went wrong. Various other Thai government representatives, local civic leaders and medical personnel had also promised to attend.

It wasn't quite the experiment Edgar Pask had conducted on himself, but it still sounded to me like an excellent idea, and it had clearly been thought out down to the minutest detail. The young volunteers would be dressed in wetsuits and buoyancy vests, just as the Wild Boars would be for the actual rescue. Each boy would have a cylinder full of oxygen strapped to his front and held in place with a modified harness that had a handle on the back for an escort diver to control the unconscious boy. A lead weight in the front pocket of the harness would keep the boy face down. That was the idea, anyway.

From their own collection and from other divers at the site, the Brits had gathered a variety of face masks in different sizes – small, smaller and smallest – which they hoped to fit on the different-sized boys.

The divers would test the masks, test the tanks, test the hoses, test the silicone seals and test anything else they could think of. Rick said he would ask his young test subjects to remain perfectly still in the water, as if they were fast asleep. He said he especially wanted to see how they would breathe inside a full face mask the first time their faces were pressed into the water. 'Will they know instinctively to breathe or not?' Rick asked.

The anaesthetised seal had known how to breathe. Would the boys?

'That all sounds brilliant,' Craig said to Rick and Jason after they had laid it out for us. The swimming-pool dress rehearsal was a smart idea. It could very well teach us all some lessons that would prove lifesaving later on.

'I'll be eager to hear the results of the experiment,' I said.

Jason saw his opening there. 'So come along,' he said. 'Get up in the morning. Take a bit of a dive in the cave.

Go halfway in to make sure you feel comfortable with your gear and everything. Then meet us at the pool.'

It was a good suggestion, but I didn't think I could budge.

Craig and I would have happily gone back to the pool *after* we had scoped out the inside of the cave, had there been time. In fact, I had already raised the idea of a full dress rehearsal in a pool, including anaesthesia – no more volunteers *pretending* to be asleep.

The ethics of this were sketchy at best, but the Thai military was prepared to sanction it. They even told me they would recruit the 'volunteers' who would be sedated. But the pressure to get the rescue started and the looming threat of rain made that seem unlikely, if not impossible. We just couldn't risk another day's delay.

'This isn't really negotiable for me,' I said finally to Rick and the others. 'I have to be sure I can dive the cave before I can agree to do anything. I don't know how long the dive is, how well I will do in there. I have to see the state the kids are in. How big or little they are. How healthy or frail. I need to see the exact spot where I'm supposed to anaesthetise them. I have to work out in my own mind whether it's even possible in conditions like these.'

Only then could I agree with a clear conscience that a sedated dive was the best option.

'All right,' Jason said. 'You and Craig do your dive tomorrow. While you're at the cave, we'll have a play-around in the pool.'

What's at stake

On the drive back to the hotel that night, Michael Costa, our diligent DFAT minder, said he had something he needed to mention to us.

'In the interest of full disclosure,' he said somewhat stiffly, 'I have to tell you that if something goes wrong with the children, it's not impossible that you could get caught up in the Thai judicial system.'

'The Thai judicial system?' I repeated slowly, making sure I'd heard him right. 'You mean prison?'

He managed a stiff chuckle and said: 'Well, not exactly.'

The Australian government, Michael explained, had applied to the Thai government for diplomatic immunity for Craig and me while we were working on the rescue. That way, if anything bad should occur, we wouldn't be held legally liable. But no one could say for certain when – or even *if* – the immunity might be granted.

This made no sense to me. Hadn't Craig and I *volunteered* to come to Thailand and help these desperate children? We'd be risking our own lives trying to free them from the cave. And we were far from the only ones. There were hundreds of other kind-hearted volunteers who'd come from almost every country you could name. They were military, civilian, foreign, Thai. With the finest of intentions, they too were here to help.

'What about all these other blokes?' I asked.

'No,' Michael said, shaking his head. 'Mainly you. You're the doctor, and you'll be giving the drugs. So if the children die . . .' He let the sentence taper off there, but I was pretty sure I caught his drift. There weren't going to be any thanks-for-trying citations if something unfortunate occurred. There'd be a cosy cell in a Thai prison waiting for me. I had never been incarcerated and didn't really know anyone who had, but with everything else already swirling in my head, I now had the pleasure of imagining what and who might be waiting for me in my cell.

'Are you sure about all this?' I asked Michael.

I was not happy. I had accepted this high-profile mission. I had recruited my good friend Craig. I had put us both on the line. There had never been any guarantee of success. In fact, I wasn't at all sure that something wouldn't go wrong. Swimming sedated children out of a flooded cave was not a foolproof plan. *If the Thais have a better alternative, please, by all means, grab it! I'll bow out and let some other idiot swim in there.*

That was what I was thinking; that wasn't what I said. Instead of erupting like a volcano, I shrugged.

'You know what, Michael?' I said. 'I've got too much to think about already. You've got to take care of this. So let's not speak of it again.'

He just stared.

'Seriously,' I said, 'I can't think about this right now. You'll just have to look after me if something goes wrong, okay? Scoop me up. Get me out of Thailand. I trust you. I'm in your hands.'

Michael promised he would take care of Craig and me if anything went horribly wrong. At least that's the way I heard it, but I had no plans to test his promise. It was late and we were both totally knackered. What a day! We had a dive planned for the morning into a dark and difficult cave.

III
DIVING

11
FIRST DIP
CRAIG

We had studied Vern's map of the cave, of course, and a couple of others too. But a map is only the roughest estimation, the vaguest notion of what you'll find inside a cave. No piece of paper, not even a beautifully shot video, can adequately capture the infinite variables inside a cave. The clarity of the water. The hues of the limestone. The sound of the echoes. The heaviness of the air. The size, shape and difficulty of the restrictions. The vital importance of the guide line, without which you're lost.

I don't care if you're the next Leonardo da Vinci. There is no way to draw that on a map.

Be prepared

Since this was Thailand in early July and we figured the water would be relatively warm, Harry and I climbed into thin surfing wetsuits – *squeezed* into the suit, in Harry's case. (Sorry, mate.) We had fins, dive harnesses with built-in buoyancy, and various accessories – spare lights, carabiners, extra reels for emergencies – clipped onto D-rings. No full face masks for us, just normal regulators. Each of us carried three side-mounted eleven-litre air cylinders – eighty-eights, we call them – two on one side, one on the other. Three is more than we would normally carry. That slows you down a bit. But this time, we went with the added margin of safety. We wouldn't be able to rescue anyone if we had our own catastrophe inside the cave. This dive had to go well.

Actually, 'this dive' isn't the best way to put it. It was seven shorter dives, separated by air chambers that we swam or waded through. The tanks alone weighed nearly twenty kilos each – a lot of lugging there. Fortunately, a guide line was already in place to lead us in and out of the cave.

Much of the line was climbing rope. Normally, cave divers use braided string, around 3 millimetres in diameter, to mark their route into the cave, so anyone using it will have a clear path out. But Rick, John and Ben had put some line in. They had wisely decided to use the fatter climbing rope, stronger than regular line. They knew that quite a few people would be coming and going from the cave, and not just experienced cave divers. That climbing rope was sure to get an absolute flogging, but it wasn't going to break no matter how many untrained amateurs yanked on it. If they'd used normal braided line, it would already have been in tatters or pulled loose for sure.

Around 11 a.m., Harry and I carried our gear to the entrance of the cave, trying not to attract attention as we wove through the mob of people who were milling around. The crowd had definitely grown in the twenty-something hours since we had arrived.

'Here goes,' Harry said as we made our way into the first chamber of the cave without anyone stopping or even recognising us.

'Let's do it,' I replied.

There isn't much talking on a cave dive. There is none underwater, and not much more at the surface, while you are grunting and struggling into the current. Sporadic cussing is about it, which leaves hand and light signals, and the occasional tap or nudge, nod or head jerk. This is part of what makes cave diving such a solo sport, even when it's done in teams.

Setting out

The first half-kilometre was a hike along a stream, over some rocks and hills, up steep slopes slick with mud and the drippings of other workers and divers. As we secured our masks and stepped into the water, it was just as warm as we had expected – about 23 degrees Celsius. Some of the local divers had said that the water felt cold to them. But given a few of the frigid places Harry and I had gone diving over the years, it didn't feel the least bit chilly to us. We were in a section called a roof sniff, where the water almost reaches the ceiling and if you want to keep breathing you must haul yourself through with your nose in the air, like a dog swimming. That's when we reached the first sump. It wasn't long at all, ten quick metres between chambers 2 and 3, but it gave us a clear warning of things to come. We had to slide through a tight flattener – a section in which our backs touched the rock above while our chests were touching the rock below. It was only short, but tight enough that, as Harry and I passed through, you could hear our cylinders clanging against the rock. It's amazing how clearly that sound cuts through water, like an urgently ringing doorbell on a silent night.

All I could think of as we were banging through was how much harder this would be towing a sedated boy. It was tough enough for Harry and me on our own; it would be a whole lot tougher with an unconscious passenger.

The passage narrowed there, concentrating the myriad water pipes, communications and power cables that had been brought into the cave. It was a chaotic tangle of artificial and natural obstacles. But at the far end of that tight underwater passage was its geological opposite – a huge open chamber.

A steep, gooey mud slope led up to chamber 3, as spacious as a train station, and bustling with activity. It was where the stranded Thai water workers had been found. It was also the dive base for the entire rescue mission, a combination warehouse, dormitory, repair shop, relief station and rec hall where divers, technicians, soldiers and assorted support personnel supplied and inventoried almost everything that went in or out of the cave. A large group of Thai Navy SEALs were living there, with sleeping-bags, plastic bottles of water, and military rations to eat. They had their own communications gear and, apparently, they'd run a fibre-optic internet line in there. Stacked inside chamber 3 were probably 300 dive cylinders. I could hardly believe my eyes when I saw that mountain of tanks. It looked like an untidy Bunnings. I half-expected someone to ask me, 'What aisle are the showerheads in?' For divers like us, heading deeper into the cave, chamber 3 was an oasis.

But our reconnaissance journey had only begun. 'Ready for a nice spot of cave diving?' Harry asked me with a smile. Standard cave-diver sarcasm.

I nodded, returning the grin.

We'd been warned about the section between chamber 3 and chamber 4. This was where the former Thai Navy SEAL, Saman Gunan, had died. Once we reached that spot, it was easy to understand how.

A cruel obstacle course

This section was by far the worst part of the cave to dive through – 150 metres long, and extremely difficult to navigate. Rocks projecting from the roof kept cracking against our helmets, even as we tried to anticipate them by waving our hands in front of our faces. There was a T in the line where someone had taken an early wrong turn, up into a tiny air chamber with a blind ending. We had to return to the T-junction to find the right way to go. A tricky S-bend through a vertical slit meant we had to slide ourselves through a 3D puzzle that could only be solved by trial and error in the inky blackness of the water. Finally, there was a classic line trap, where the rope had been pulled into a gap so narrow that it was impossible for a diver to follow. We held the rope at arm's length while we groped around in the dark to find a larger hole that would accommodate our girth. Yep, this section was like a cruel obstacle course designed by the most malevolent cave-diving instructor ever!

'Boy, I wouldn't want to be bringing a kid through there,' Harry said after we'd cleared it. 'That was tight for me on my own.'

But we kept moving, partly by swimming, partly by wading. In places, it was easier just to pull yourself along the rope hand-over-hand. That seemed to be the most efficient way to travel. Overall, it would be another kilometre and a half like that. While the water was coming towards us, we had a couple of metres' visibility. Not good but not too bad – for now. On the way out, the visibility would be close to zero, after we'd stirred up the mud deeper in the cave. Seeing would be a good deal harder.

There was a spot, about halfway to the boys, that the British divers had told us to look out for. Monk's Junction, it was called on the map. 'It's where the tunnel separates,' Rick said. 'You'll know you're there because all of a sudden, clear, warm water is coming through from the right. You're swimming along through so-so visibility, then the water gets warmer and you can see. It's just for a few metres, but it's noticeable.'

Rick had it exactly right.

Normal temperature, blah visibility, a fork in the tunnel, then – *whoosh!* For a few sweet metres, warm, clear water came rushing in.

As experienced divers, Harry and I knew that meant fresh water was flowing in from a tributary. The warm, clear water quickly mixed with the muck and faded to nothingness, but it would be a hard-to-miss halfway marker every time we came and went. By comparison, most of the rest of the route, with the exception of chamber 3 and a couple of tight, nasty crawls, was fairly forgettable, no matter how closely we studied the map or how many times we'd pass through. Sump, air chamber, sump, air chamber. But there was no missing Monk's Junction.

Our anxiety grew as we got ever closer to the boys. It was one thing to make rescue plans at a distance. It would be something else to look them in the eye and explain to them exactly what we had in mind. The rescue was getting more real with every rope pull.

After a while, it was hard to know how close we were to our goal. Each time we surfaced into a dry patch or an air chamber, one or the other of us would wonder: *Are we there yet?* You lose track of how far you've come. We tried to stay alert for certain landmarks. At one spot, we were told, the orange rope would change to flat black tape, and then back to orange rope again. Near the end, there'd be a stretch of thin blue rope. Once we hit the blue rope, we'd know we were close to chamber 9 and the kids.

People had mentioned chamber 4 and chamber 6 and chamber 7. But we'd come up and down, up and down. We didn't know exactly where we were. Some of the sumps were chest-deep, and we waded along, pulling on the rope. But half the time, we didn't even know whether there was rock above us, or air, or what we had in front of us.

Once we reached chambers 7 and 8, we had to climb out of the water and walk. We kept our tanks on, but took off our masks and fins and carried them. Gravity sucks when you are carrying gear along a sandy beach and up over rocks.

Again, the thought kept intruding: *How will this be for those who are carrying the boys?*

Quite a pretty dive

The last sump we passed through, about 300 metres long, was by far the nicest bit in the cave. This was more like the cave diving we enjoy rather than the slog we had just experienced. It was actually quite a pretty dive in that section, a nice refresher before the main event.

Then we reached the thin blue rope.

Rick and John had warned us about the stench in chamber 9.

'As soon as we stuck our heads up,' Rick had said, 'it was putrid in there.'

This made sense. The boys had been in the cave for two weeks by then producing plenty of human waste. Have you ever been inside a high-school locker room? That's what I was expecting to swim into.

As we surfaced, I didn't smell anything, but I don't have the greatest sense of smell.

'Smells like ammonia,' Harry said. 'Acrid. Is that urine?'

We had emerged into what turned out to be quite a long canal. There was still no sign of the boys. We kept swimming along the surface with our masks on, keeping a hand on the rope and inching forward. Finally, on the left, a partly flooded beach came into view. Low. Sandy. Flat. On the right was a ledge. The deep canal dividing them ran on, disappearing into the distance up ahead.

We'd been told there was a beach opposite where the kids were. 'You'll see a hill going up,' John had told us. 'They're up there.' Once we saw the beach, we knew it wouldn't be much longer. By that point, our general unease had risen to genuine anxiety. How would the boys respond when we explained the dicey plan we had in mind for them?

'Anything's possible,' Harry said. Perhaps we'd read too many books about people trapped on desert islands, where the rescuers were often tomorrow's lunch.

We stopped at the beach, shed the tanks there and pulled off our fins. We knew we had some climbing in front of us. Then we paddled across the water with our masks on. As we glided across the surface, we began to hear voices, just as predicted, off to the right and up ahead. We saw lights. Then we saw people. They were waving. At us.

12

WILD BOARS

HARRY

'G'day,' I called to the waving boys as I pulled myself out of the water. 'Hello,' Craig said.

'Hi!' the boys called back. It was possible that was all the English most of them knew, aside from a few other stray words.

Now that Craig and I had survived the gruelling two-and-a-half-kilometre dive, there were several pieces of business to attend to. First of all, we needed to observe the stranded boys. I wanted to see whether they were really as healthy as I'd heard. I didn't expect to perform full medical examinations – that would have been impossible on such a tight deadline, with no medical equipment and in dismal light – but I wanted to make my own assessment. I also needed to make some initial calculations about how much ketamine I would need for each of the boys, assuming we pressed ahead and got permission to proceed. I would have to use enough of the drug to ensure each boy stayed unconscious for a good while but not so much that anyone would stop breathing underwater or take too long to recover after the journey out. These were children, after all. I didn't want to drug them any more deeply than I had to. Getting the dosages right would be one of the most difficult judgements I'd have to make: heavier doses for the larger children, smaller doses for the little ones. Size mattered, but there'd still be plenty of guesswork involved.

I also wanted to scope out a precise location for my make-do operating theatre. And I was eager to make friends with the Thai Navy SEALs who had been caring for the boys and the Army medic leading the team, Dr Pak Loharnshoon. Several people had mentioned him, sounding impressed. We would need the military doctor and his men as allies to explain to the children in Thai what was about to happen to them, and do it in a way that wouldn't make them freak out or refuse to cooperate.

First contact

When Craig and I reached the bottom of the hill, two of the boys had already scampered down to meet us. They must have been the greeting party. The others were still up on the ledge. That slope looked pretty steep to me. It was muddy and slippery and wet. Not that the kids seemed to mind. They were light, and their bare feet were tiny. They dug their toes into the mud and kept their balance as they trotted down that hill.

As we scrambled up the slope behind them, slipping and sliding and lurching about, their sure-footedness made us feel even more like the middle-aged men we were.

Some kind people – the British divers? the Thai SEALs? – had installed a rope to steady the climb, which helped a little, but we were puffing and panting and still made fools of ourselves. The kids found the whole thing hilarious.

Headlights came on as we reached the top. Some of the kids were curled up in space blankets, possibly asleep – it was a little like invading their secret camp site. But there was no mistaking the thrill in the air. They were delighted to see us, and we were happy to be there.

After we finally got to the top, the boys came over to greet us, bowing and smiling as they made the traditional *wai* gesture – palms together, chin to thumb, as if praying. A couple of the SEALs came to greet us too. We were all bowing and smiling and shaking hands – firm, solid grips all around – when a voice came out of the darkness, clear and strong.

'Hello there.'

Dr Pak

The voice belonged to a fit young Thai man with a close-cropped military haircut and a hundred-watt smile. He was Dr Pak – the Royal Thai Army doctor (and lieutenant colonel) supervising the Navy medical team. We would discover that Pak had completed just about every training program the Thai military had to offer, besides the Navy SEAL course, and was certified for Airborne, Recon, Special Forces, Rangers, Commandos, Parajumpers and the Queen's Guard. If the Thai military did it, chances are Pak did it too – and might well be the chief instructor for next year's course. He also commanded the Army's 3rd Medical Battalion in Nakhon Ratchasima province, north-east of Bangkok. Put it like this: if I had to be trapped in a cave with no certain release date, I'd definitely want Dr Pak looking after me. The man oozed calm and confidence. He had a physician's caring demeanour and a military officer's complete-the-mission attitude.

The doctor's English wasn't perfect, but it was good enough to communicate and far superior to our non-existent Thai. We spoke slowly, and so did he. 'I'm Harry,' I said. 'This is Craig.' I explained that I was a doctor from Australia and that we were eager to learn about the health of the boys.

Pak seemed happy to oblige. 'Overall,' he said, 'they are in far better condition than I expected. They are all fully conscious. Some minor concerns, but no serious issues. I would say all of them are healthy.'

Amazing.

It was much the same report we'd got from the British divers. Now a physician was saying it too. Given what these boys had been through, could they really be in such terrific shape?

Before we discussed that further, Pak showed us around the camp site, which was now being shared by all seventeen of them – the twelve boys, Coach Ekk and the four members of the Thai military. Conditions were still rough, but they'd improved, the doctor said, as food and other supplies were brought in. Along with the blankets and the torches, there was now a ready store of fruit drinks, energy bars and US Army ready-to-eat meals or MREs. No more drinking the questionable cave water. That had been replaced by plastic bottles of fresh water, and a filtration pump brought in by the Thais.

As we spoke with Pak, several of the boys lingered nearby, listening to our conversation, though I don't believe many of them could understand more than a few words. Then one boy, who seemed particularly friendly, approached and spoke to us in English.

'How are you? My name is Adul. What is your name? Welcome to our home in the cave.'

When I praised his English, Adul said he also knew Thai, Burmese, Mandarin and Wa, a language spoken near the border between Myanmar and China. 'I translate for the others if you like,' he said.

Now, that could come in handy.

I returned my attention to Pak. He became animated talking about Ekk, and how the team's young assistant coach had led and calmed the boys. 'He is a strong and soothing influence,' the Thai doctor said.

Coach Ekk

Ekk had told him that on the first two nights they'd been stuck in the cave, emotions ran dangerously high. The boys were crying and upset. Several of them seemed certain they would never see their families or friends again. But the coach had called on his training as a novice monk. He led the boys in group meditation, which they happily participated in, partly because he'd invited them to, and partly to ease the boredom of the cave. That seemed to calm the boys, and brought the team together and lowered the tension for everyone, Pak said.

The youngest boy, Titan, was terribly scared of the darkness. Ekk kept a special eye on him each night. Though there was zero natural light in the cave, just the torches and the dim glow of the boys' watches, it seemed that their own diurnal rhythms did still make them feel more sleepy at 'night'.

At Coach Ekk's direction, Pak said, the boys had dug a hole into the wall of the cave. It went a good three or four metres. 'The coach didn't really think they could crawl all the way to safety,' Pak said with a smile. 'But he understood it would give them hope, and something to keep them occupied. They needed both of those.'

Pak told us the coach had done everything he could think of to find a way out. The attempt he'd made on the first night they were trapped was especially valiant.

Ekk had tied a rope around his waist, handing the other end to three of the older boys – Tee, Adul and Night. He then climbed into the water, swimming as far as he could in hope of finding an underwater passage. They had a signal worked out in advance.

'If I run out of breath and I can't go any further, I will pull the rope two times. Two times. Then you must pull me back as quickly as you can.'

Now, *that* was a bold plan. Craig and I were amazed at such ingenuity and bravery. But that was only half the tale.

'If I do not pull on the rope,' the young coach had told the boys, 'you will know that I have passed safely through the opening. If I can make it, everybody can.'

The boys had smiled at that, Pak said. Their coach had a game plan.

Ekk held the rope tightly. He stepped into the murky water and waded into the current, which, he told Pak, had been surprisingly stiff. He took a deep breath, the deepest breath he could, filling his lungs with air. He put his head into the water, then pulled himself into the flooded passages with his hands and feet. He didn't swim exactly, just pulled himself underwater. He could feel the hard rock above his head and soft sand at his toes. He couldn't see anything. The opening was smaller than he had imagined. But he was skinny, and he thought he could fit through.

Ekk kept moving as fast and far as he was able to, constantly bumping against the rocks. When he could go no further, when he felt almost out of air, Ekk knew he had to turn back.

The story was truly riveting. Ekk's extraordinary attempt to save the boys was an incredible window into what they'd already gone through. Then came the climax.

Unable to hold his breath underwater any longer, Ekk gave the rope two strong pulls and held on tightly. The boys didn't hesitate. Frantically, they hauled him in. He was back with them in just a few seconds. By then, he was gasping for air.

'That way won't work,' Ekk told the boys reluctantly. 'We will find a new way. That is what we will do.'

Good grief! I thought.

'To me,' the doctor added, 'Coach Ekk is almost a saint.'

The young man hadn't just inspired the boys and kept them focused – he'd been willing to risk his life for them.

I looked around, trying to find him among the boys, but I couldn't. At twenty-five, Coach Ekk was a decade older than some of his players, but good luck picking him out of the group. There wasn't much difference between him and some of the older boys. Rick and John had told us the assistant coach looked so young that he could pass for a teenager.

With the camera mounted on my helmet, I shot some video of the boys, waving, smiling, saying hello to their parents and going about their business in the cave. They were all so cheerful and upbeat, it was easy to forget they were stranded in a situation that could very well have cost them their lives and might still. It was almost like they were sending home greetings from school camp.

Letters from home

I had brought along several messages with me in a waterproof pouch. One was a letter in Thai from a high-ranking Navy commander to Dr Pak and the SEAL team. The others were from the boys' families, and would be quoted verbatim in the media all around the world within twenty-four hours.

These were the parents' responses to the notes that the boys had sent out the previous day with Jason and Chris.

The boys began to read.

Dear Mark, know that Mummy is waiting for you in front of the cave. I miss you, and please don't feel bad. Mother Hom loves you a lot, and please take good care of yourself.

Dear Biw, Daddy and Mummy miss you. Love you always.

The messages alternated between optimism and heartbreak. But in the brief back-and-forth, you could clearly hear the boys trying to calm their parents and the parents trying to calm the boys. Without a doubt, these children were loved.

Dear Nick, please take care of yourself. Daddy and Mummy are waiting for you. – Father Be, Mother Nang and Nong Bonus

I didn't know who these people were, but I'll bet Nick was delighted hearing from them.

On every page were little snatches of these families' lives. In the note from his parents, Night's postponed birthday came up again.

Dad and Mum are waiting to arrange your birthday party. Please get out soon, and stay healthy. Mummy knows that you can do it. And you must not be too worried about it. Daddy and Mummy, as well as Grandfather, Grandmother and all the relatives, are supporting you always. Daddy and Mummy love you so much. – Father Boon, Mother O

One note explained that Mick's grandfather couldn't write properly, so someone had helped him to draft a few lines.

Dear Nong Mick, Grandfather Lek is waiting at the cave's entrance. Grandfather Lek hopes that Mick gets really healthy, and Mick must not be afraid of anyone's condemning him. Grandfather Lek is never angry at you. Grandfather Lek loves Mick always. – Grandfather Lek

Since Tee's and Dom's parents both had to leave the cave site temporarily to look after their businesses, they had asked a social worker to write notes for them.

Tee and Dom, [your] dads and mums wish you safety. The mental health team told us that your dads and mums have strong health. We wish you strong spirit and to come out. We are waiting for you at the cave's entrance.

Tern's mother wrote a note to all of the boys:

Dear children, Now every parent is waiting and supporting you. We are not angry at you. Please, take good care of yourselves and cover up with blankets. It's cold, and I'm worried about you boys. You will be out in a short time. Daddy Sak and Mother Ae are waiting for you. – Patchanee Takhamsong (Mother Ae)

Like their fourteen-year-old son, Adul's parents were not Thai Buddhists but stateless Christians, followers of the Baptist faith, and they told him they missed him and were praying for him:

Father and Mother want to see your face. Father and Mother pray for you and your friends in order to see you soon. After you leave the cave, we want you to say thank you to every official. We want you to trust in God. No worries, Father and Mother will be waiting until you come out.

Like many others, Adul's parents added an extra note of support for the team's assistant coach:

Thank you for taking care of the children, and leading the children to safety when they were staying in the dark. Return to the bosom of your father and mother on the outside. We are waiting outside with love and care too.

Titan's mum also included a shout-out to the coach in her note to her son:

Titan, be strong. I love you. I care about you. I'm cheering you up! I'm waiting for you in front of the cave. Bring all the boys, Ekk.

Note's and Pong's parents took a similar approach, sprinkled with parental concern

Dear Note, Father and Mother are waiting. Take good care of yourself. Father Neung and Mother Dao miss you a lot. Please tell Coach Ekk not to be too worried. Mother is not angry at him. – Rattanadao Chantapoon

Dear Pong, please take care of your health and stay strong. Father, Mother and everyone are waiting outside to welcome you back to us safely. I would like to thank you, Coach Ekk, for taking care of our twelve children. Coach, please don't be worried. Every parent thanks you for taking care of our children. Daddy and Mummy are waiting to welcome you. – Father Chai and Mother Orn

Coach Ekk's aunt also wrote. She started out like many of the other relatives, but she also reminded her nephew that the boys and their families all loved him and didn't blame him for the ordeal, and that he should please stay strong:

Top left: L-R: Geoff Paynter, Richard Harris, Ken Smith, Craig Challen, John Currie, Simon Doughty and Mark Brown. At the finish of the 2008 Cocklebiddy expedition after extending the known cave for the first time since 1995. *Photo by Geoff Paynter*

Top right: Harry with his father, James Dunbar Harris, in Whangarei, New Zealand, in 1997.

On our expedition with the Wet Mules diving group in China. Behind Harry and Craig lies the Daxing Spring, which the team dived to 213m depth. *Photo by Heather Endall*

Shortly after everyone was safely out of the cave successfully, Prime Minister Malcolm Turnbull spoke to the Australian rescuers on a Skype call, which was set up in a tiny hotel room.

Our interpreter, Kittanu Supasamsen, or Nu for short. Nu's job usually involved getting rowdy Australians out of jail, so the cave rescue was a new adventure for him.
Photo by Richard Harris

Harry giving the rescue team a lesson in Anaesthesia 101.

Craig and Harry back at the surface after a day in the cave.

Craig in the ambulance during the 'escape' from meeting the Thai prime minister, accompanied by Kittanu and the Thai medical and nursing staff.

As Harry disembarks from the plane in Chiang Rai, the body of Saman Gunan is loaded into the Thai Navy aircraft on the right. A military parade gives Saman a send-off. *Photo by Richard Harris*

Above: The boy is asleep, his full face mask is on and Chris Jewell is strapping the cylinder to his chest. In the background, Rick and John await their turns. *Photo by Richard Harris.*

Above: L–R: The Star of Courage (the second highest Australian civilian award for bravery), Knights Grand Cross (First Class) of the Order of the Direkgunabhorn and the Medal of the Order of Australia (OAM). *Photo by Richard Harris.*

Above: At the top of the steep slope in chamber 9, the boys await their turn to escape the cave. *Below:* Only their lights can be seen. On the slope itself Dr Pak (rear) and a Navy SEAL chat with Harry.

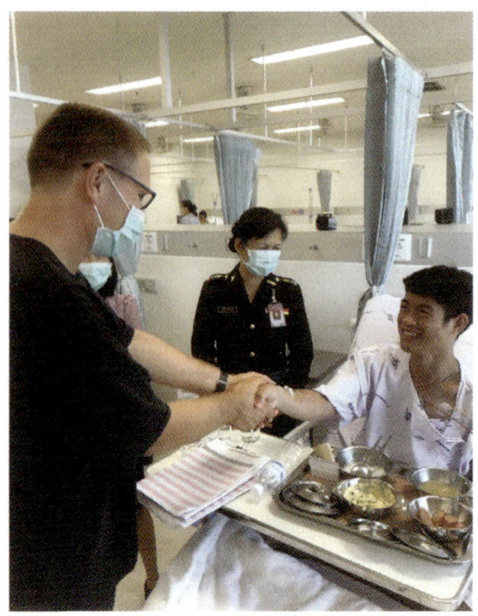

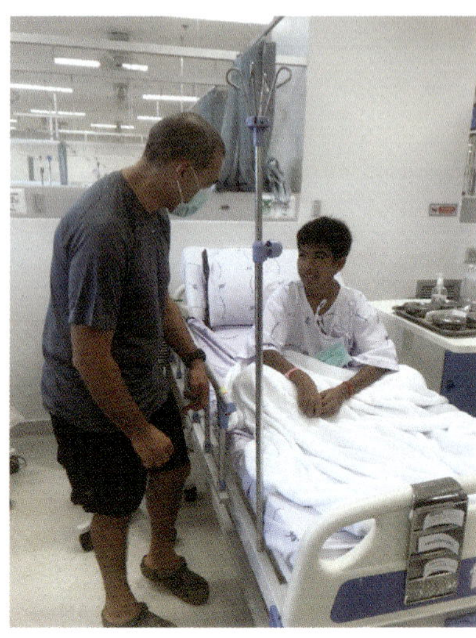

Above: Harry greeting Coach Ekk (left) and Craig with one of the older boys (right) in the hospital after the successful rescue mission.

Below: Meeting young Titan in the hospital after the rescue. Always smiling!

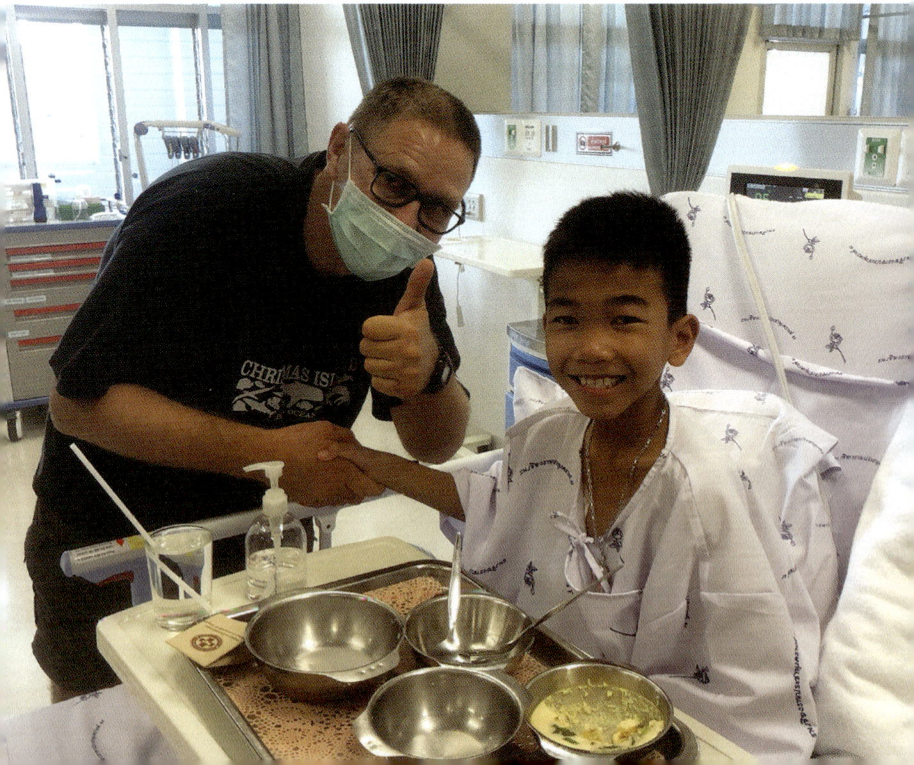

Nine months after the rescue, Craig and Harry visit six of the Wild Boars boys and Coach Ekk at a temple in Thailand.

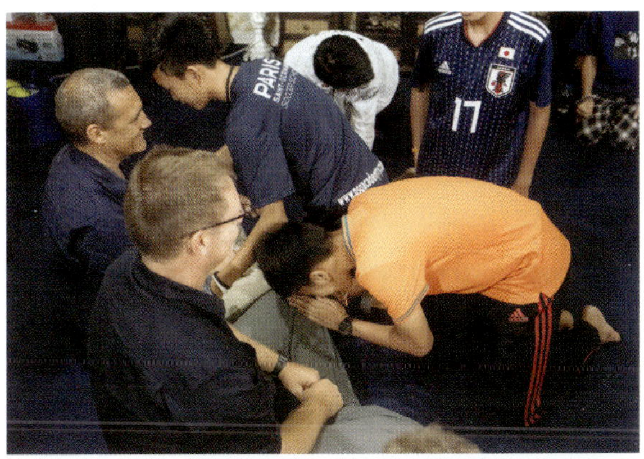

Reunited with two of their rescuers, the boys take turns kneeling in front of Craig and Harry, bowing and resting their head a moment on the divers' knees, before getting up and sharing a hug.

John Volanthen, Rick Stanton and Craig relax at Le Méridien Chiang Rai resort. *Photo by Richard Harris*

An honour: Harry receiving the Edgar Pask Citation from Dr Kathleen Ferguson on behalf of the Association of Anaesthetists of Great Britain and Ireland in London, December 2018.

Craig and Harry after being awarded Australians of the Year 2019. *Photo by Mick Tsikas/AAP*

Clockwise from left: Matthew Fitzgerald, Troy Eather, Justin Bateman, Robert James, Christopher Markcrow, Kelly Boers, Benjamin Cox, Craig Challen and Richard Harris, standing with bravery medals they received for their roles in the rescue. *Photo by Sean Davey/AAP*

Harry and Craig meeting Their Royal Highnesses the Duke and Duchess of Sussex at Admiralty House during their Royal Tour of Australia. *Photo courtesy Government House*

I'm waiting for you in front of the cave. Don't worry too much. Take care of yourself. No one blames you. I urge you to keep fighting. I'm cheering you up. I miss you. No one blames you. Many people are giving you moral support. Keep fighting. I love you. Bring all the boys out. Keep fighting.

Lest there be any doubt about the parents' feelings towards Coach Ekk, several others wrote to him directly, mixing their concern for their children with encouragement for the young man:

Dear Coach Ekk, the parents of every child have asked you to take care of our children. Please, don't blame yourself for this. We want you to rest assured that every parent is not upset or angry at you, and everybody understands and supports you. Thank you very much for taking care of our children. You went into the cave with our children, and you must get out with them. Take our children (and yourself) out with safety. We are waiting in front of the cave.

When the boys were finished reading, it was obvious what an uplifting experience it had been for them to receive these letters. I knew how relieved the parents had been, receiving the notes that Jason and Chris had brought out on Friday. I wanted to keep this correspondence going. I figured we might as well give it another round. If the boys wrote replies, Craig and I could carry the notes back out with us.

I passed around a couple of pads. 'Write something,' I said. 'Write something to your parents.'

With some quick translation from Adul and Pak, the boys began scribbling again.

If anything, our short visit with the boys seemed to have energised them. I was happy that they were happy, but it was still strange. Did they understand what terrible danger they were in? Did they know that even those planning to rescue them lacked confidence in the rescue plan? So much smiling in the face of so much peril.

I ran Pak through a basic health survey. The boys, who'd gone entirely without food for nine days and had been subsisting on brought-in rations ever since, all looked super thin to me. Maybe not as emaciated as some of the most sensational media coverage had implied, but very thin.

'Do any of them have diarrhoea?' 'Is anyone vomiting?'

'Any of them seem particularly weak?'

'Do any have skin irritations that you're worried about?' 'Coughing? Chest infections?'

'There is some coughing,' Pak said. But with a couple of minor exceptions, he answered every other question with an unequivocal *no*. 'They're all good,' he said. 'Morale is high. Things have improved very much since the boys got food. The food is all from America. Steaks. Pasta. Beans. Crackers. They never ate this kind of food before. They really like it!'

I could hear a couple of moist coughs in the dim light of the cave. That could mean a minor chest cold, or it could mean full-blown pneumonia. Hard to say. Without a proper examination, I had no way of knowing for sure.

Before we came into the cave, I had asked a Thai doctor to help me write a short summary of the rescue plan, as clear and simple as we could make it. Enough to lay out the basics for the boys but not enough to alarm anyone.

Sharing the plan

'I have something I'd like you to read out loud,' I said to Pak. 'It's in Thai. It describes a plan for rescuing the boys. I want them all to know what will be happening, how we will try to get them out. I don't want anyone to be surprised. We are hoping to start tomorrow.'

I handed Pak the paper. He summoned all the boys, who gathered around him as he read. The first and only words I recognised were 'Dr Harry' and 'Dr Craig'. But as he read on, a horrible thought occurred to me. *I really hope he doesn't stop halfway through this letter and say: 'You've got to be kidding! You're going to do what? Sedate them and dive them out underwater? This is madness. You know it'll be a death sentence for every one of them.'*

I definitely didn't want him making a fuss in front of these children. Goodness knows how badly they might be spooked. It would put them in the worst possible frame of mind, just when we needed their cooperation, as the rescue was set to begin.

But Pak did no such thing. About halfway through, he shot me a glance, perfectly businesslike, and then read on.

I could only imagine what he was thinking. He had every right to. *You guys must be crazy. What medical book did you get this one from? All these experts from around the world! Is this the best that you can do?*

I'd probably agree with most of it. But it was the best we could do – it was the only real option.

Pak just kept reading.

Though I couldn't understand what he was saying, that didn't matter. I was far more interested in the boys' reactions. What was going through their minds?

He read. They listened. I watched.

I looked from boy to boy, from face to face, for some kind of sign. It was only then that I really started to suspect just how tough and resilient these kids were – or how keen they were to get out of there.

Many of them were nodding. Several smiled. A couple of them gave the thumbs-up sign. Not one of them looked the slightest bit like he was going to whimper or cry or collapse in hysterics. They all just took it on board with a shrug: *Yep, sounds like an excellent plan.* None of them looked at all afraid. These kids were prepared to do whatever it took to get out of this cave.

'When you wake up, you will be outside the cave.' That's what Pak had told the boys at the end of his presentation, as I'd find out later. The Thai doctor on the outside had written that last line a little differently. 'You will wake up in the hospital,' he wrote. Apparently, Pak had decided that ending might be too frightening for the boys. So he did a little editing on the fly.

It amazed me how natural Pak seemed with the boys. Though he was obviously a high-ranking military officer, he didn't seem the least bit intimidating. Maybe it was the doctor in him – or the dad. Even before he told me, I knew Pak had to be a father.

'You've got a good way with these kids,' I told him.

'Thank you,' he said. 'They are good children. They

make my job easier. Do you have children, Dr Harry?'

'My wife and I have three,' I said. 'But they're older than these little blokes.'

'I have one,' he said. 'My little boy. When I look at these boys, the smaller ones especially, I can't help it, I see my son. What if something happened to him?'

'Did he know you were coming here?'

'My wife, she knew,' Pak said. 'I told her I would be home in two or three days.'

'I think you're going to be late for dinner,' I said.

'Very late,' he agreed. 'I hope I have not given her too many reasons to worry.'

Preparations

Before Craig and I said our goodbyes and headed back out of the cave for the night, we had some practical instructions for Pak to follow. If the plan earned final approval from the Thai authorities, we would need him to help prepare the boys for their sedation and the journey out without frightening them.

'We expect to be back tomorrow at midday,' I told Pak. 'Please fast six children from six a.m.,' I continued. 'No food or drink after six. When I call for the first child, I want you to give him an alprazolam tablet to make him feel a bit sleepy and relaxed before the dive. We'll have some more wetsuits for them – masks, cylinders, everything they'll need for the journey.'

I said that I would wait in the water at the base of the steep slope for each boy to be brought down. After a last-minute medical assessment, I would inject the boy in the thigh with a dose of atropine to decrease saliva production, a precaution that would be especially important to keep the air passages clear and prevent the boy from drowning in his own saliva. As the atropine took effect, I would inject a dose of ketamine, which would render the boy unconscious within five minutes or so.

With the help of one of the British divers, we would strap on the diving mask and attach a scuba tank to the boy's chest with rubber bungee cords. Once sedated, each child would be guided out by one of the world's most renowned cave divers, Rick, John, Jason or Chris. Dived out, swum out or carried through cave passages, depending on the terrain. Breathing steadily. Unable to panic. Being delivered safely to the field hospital outside. The child's condition would be monitored as closely as the divers could manage along the way, focusing most on the depth of sedation. At the earliest sign of consciousness, the young patient would be given a top-up shot of ketamine as needed.

Pak seemed to have no difficulty grasping any of this. I couldn't tell where he stood at this point: was the plan brilliant or crazy or bold, or, as I saw it, a combination of all three?

Maybe Pak was just happy that some other doctor was making this impossible call. Whatever the reason, he seemed to be on board.

'I will help however I can,' he said.

I told him I was deeply grateful, and we most definitely needed his assistance.

I explained that we wouldn't be able to get all twelve boys plus Coach Ekk out in a single day. We figured each trip would take three or four hours, and we needed generous spacing between each boy. We would try for six boys the first day, but getting everyone out could take two or three days.

'Come up with an order,' I told Pak. 'Let us know which of the boys you'd like us to send out first. Discuss it with the coach and the boys. You decide.'

My preference, I said, though I didn't push it, was to send a couple of the strongest ones out first, giving ourselves the greatest chance of early success. That way, maybe we could build some confidence while we honed our medical and diving moves.

'We will make an order,' Pak promised.

In this young Thai military doctor I had found an important partner, when and where I needed one most. I told Pak that I knew the boys had been in good hands, and that together we would work to get everyone out.

He smiled at that. 'Harry,' he asked, 'what do you enjoy doing when you are not here?'

As I often do, I blurted out the first thing that popped into my mind. 'I like a quiet drink.'

'That's good,' Pak answered without missing a beat. 'When we are all out, we will go for a Thai beer.'

We spoke different languages. We lived in very different lands. But there was something deeply comforting in knowing that Pak and I could both enjoy a drink.

As Craig and I said our goodbyes for the evening, all the boys were smiling and waving at us. None of them knew what we knew: that despite our seeming confidence and our studied nonchalance, the mission that we'd soon be launching was anything but foolproof.

As we strapped on our masks and our tanks and climbed back into the water for the long dive out, Rick's words echoed inside my head. 'You're going to dive to the end of the cave,' he'd said the day he'd called me at the hospital. 'You're going to see these kids. They're all looking healthy and happy and smiley. Then you're going to swim away and probably leave them all to die. Be mindful of that before you say yes with too much enthusiasm.'

I had tried to, but here we were.

'See you tomorrow,' I said, with my own studied cheerfulness. 'Big day ahead.'

I could only hope that would turn out to be true.

13
GENERAL ASSEMBLY
HARRY

It was half past seven when we climbed out of the water and half past eight when we stepped out of the cave. It was after nine by the time we returned to the British camp headquarters and got to speak with the Brits and the Americans about their swimming-pool run-through.

Practice run

How had it gone? I asked Rick.

'Brilliantly,' he beamed.

They'd tested the bungee cords and the cylinder placement. They adjusted the face masks and the buoyancy weights. They got all the gear right where they wanted it, performing flawlessly in the pool. And nothing bad had happened to any of the teenage volunteers, even when the Brits passed them from diver to diver without ever coming up for air. Everyone got safely out of the pool.

Jamie Brisbin had been key here. One of the pararescue

guys with the 31st Rescue Squadron of the US Air Force, he was also an equipment whiz. He'd stripped all the face masks, tweaked and reassembled them, securing the seals and adjusting the airflow to perfectly accommodate the special challenges of the cave environment. This came as no surprise to Craig and me. We'd got to know Jamie way back in 2009 when he'd visited Australia on a dive trip. Now he'd interrupted his family holiday in Kyoto, Japan, to be here at the cave.

'You thought I would miss this?' he asked.

Based on the pool experiment, Rick did say he wanted to make one last adjustment: binding the kids' wrists behind their backs, perhaps with cable ties and spring-loaded carabiners, and tying their ankles together with bungees. It was important for the boys to be as streamlined as possible while the divers ferried them through the cave's restricted passages and narrow openings. 'We don't want to bang anybody around unnecessarily,' Rick said.

The way he described it, we'd be wrapping the anaesthetised children into tight little packages before shipping them out of the cave – our own underwater FedEx, more or less. All that was required of the unconscious boys was to keep breathing and not to cause any trouble along the way. These precautions, Rick said, would reduce the chance of a stray arm or leg getting caught on an obstruction in the water, or injured. And if one of the boys woke up from the anaesthesia, he'd still be safely constrained.

The British divers wanted to hear our impressions of Dr Pak and the boys. I told Rick I could now understand what he meant about meeting all those smiling children and then saying goodbye, not knowing what the future had in store for them. 'Sobering,' I said.

Four at a time

We were still waiting for the green light from the Thais, but in the meantime, Rick wrote up a tentative line-up of divers for the next day, including what roles everyone would play. The first change was that we were no longer going to attempt six rescues on day one. That seemed like too many. In addition, only four really suitable full face masks had been identified that day in the pool. Instead, Rick and the other three most experienced British divers – John, Chris and Jason – would be the ones ferrying the first four boys out of the cave, each diver responsible for one boy. Other divers, including Craig, would be stationed at strategic locations inside the cave, assessing the boys' condition, keeping things moving and, when needed, giving top-ups of ketamine to any boy who seemed to be waking from his drug-induced slumber.

Two European divers, Claus Rasmussen of Denmark and Mikko Paasi of Finland, would join Craig in chamber 8. Ivan Karadzic, also from Denmark, and Canadian Erik Brown would be meeting the boys in chamber 6. They would help and support the mission in any way needed.

Craig and Rick would have special duties, a bit different from the other divers. Craig would give each boy a thorough check-up after the initial leg of the perilous underwater dive. That would be our very first chance to see if the plan could possibly work or not. Could we really dive a sedated child through a flooded cave and not kill him on the way?

Craig would be the first one to know. With his years as a veterinary surgeon, he had the skill and experience to make this crucial judgement. He knew ketamine. He knew respiration. He knew vital signs and what they might mean. Though his practice focused on animals, almost all of that knowledge applies just as well to humans. Craig was perfectly suited to the role. It would also allow him to demonstrate directly to all the other divers how to assess the health of the boys along the way and decide whether to give them a further dose.

Rick would have double-duty when the rescue finally began. He would begin the day with Craig, Claus and Mikko in chamber 8. As soon as the first boy came through and Craig completed his field assessment, Rick would swim back to me in chamber 9 and deliver an early progress report. *How did the first leg of the dive go? How does the boy look? What is Craig saying? Did the ketamine dose seem about right? What mistakes could we correct when carrying out extractions 2 to 13?* That way, Craig's assessment wouldn't just help the first boy. It would inform all of us. I would wait to hear back from Rick before sedating and sending out the second boy.

So, what were we forgetting? Would we have enough divers in the cave? We would need the help of many hands. Rick asked who else I knew.

'There are a couple of divers from Australia we could get, but I can see the DFAT guys having kittens at the very idea of asking for two more,' I said.

'Don't worry,' Rick said. 'We'll get a few more of our guys.' He mentioned Jim Warny, Connor Roe and Josh

Bratchley, rising stars a decade or two younger than we were. 'They'll be fine, and they'll be here,' Rick said to John.

Elon

While we'd been honing our rescue plan, Elon Musk had been busy too. The billionaire tech entrepreneur was back home in Bel Air, California, posting updates on Twitter.

'Some good feedback from cave experts in Thailand,' he tweeted on Saturday night Thai time, on 7 July, to his 26 million followers. 'Iterating with them on an escape pod design that might be safe enough to try. Also building an inflatable tube with airlocks. Less likely to work, given tricky contours, but great if it does.'

It was hard to know exactly who the Tesla founder was 'iterating with' and who was giving him all this 'good feedback'. Anyone we knew with cave experience seemed to be greeting Musk's escape pod and inflatable tube with raised eyebrows, often followed by a curt: 'That'll never work.' But high-profile creative geniuses aren't easily discouraged, especially those sitting high on the *Forbes* rich list with a nct worth hovering around US$20 billion. Musk was not deterred.

A bit later on Saturday, he tweeted again. 'Got more great feedback from Thailand. Primary path is basically a tiny, kid-size submarine using the liquid oxygen transfer tube of Falcon rocket as hull. Light enough to be carried by 2 divers, small enough to get through narrow gaps. Extremely robust.' And then: 'Continue to be amazed by the bravery, resilience & tenacity of kids & diving team in Thailand. Human character at its best.'

In the days and weeks to come, Musk's attempts to insert himself into the drama at the cave would become a source of debate, controversy and ridicule, resulting in plenty of media coverage, not to mention a bitter lawsuit. But for now, the actual rescue preparations were proceeding entirely without him.

Back to reality

Nothing could happen without the approval of the Thai government. Everyone understood that. As the plan slowly came together, it was Rick and John and the Americans who had been meeting with the Thais, over and over again. Mostly, Craig and I were able to sidestep it all. But after our divers' briefing late on Saturday, I got called in for a thorough grilling by the full Thai hierarchy – political, medical and military. They seemed to have a lot of questions.

The medical people spoke first. 'How did you choose the drugs?' 'Why these dosages?' 'Why alprazolam? Why not something longer acting?'

I said calmly I thought these were the best choices, but I was happy for other options to be proposed and considered. I didn't want to argue with anyone. I wanted consensus.

It was a crowded room. Besides the Thai government people and the British divers and Craig and me, we had the American military, some Chinese military, a couple of people from the AFP and some others who came from I-wasn't-sure-where. The language barrier made all this cumbersome. I spoke in English. The Thais spoke in Thai and English. Other people interpreted.

The Thai officials had a right to be sceptical. They didn't know us. Why should they trust us to handle this job? We're a mob of uninspiring-looking blokes who've arrived from all around the world. We have dodgy-looking, partially homemade dive equipment, and we're covered in mud. And we're telling you, 'Don't use your own military. We can handle this.'

If you're a Thai general, what do you do?

After a while, one of them sat up straight in his chair – even straighter than he had been sitting – and looked directly at me.

'With this rescue,' he asked in a low, gravelly voice, 'can you guarantee success?'

'Absolutely not,' I answered. 'We can pretty much guarantee that it *won't* be a total success. But there's no alternative.'

He didn't ask anything else after that.

It didn't seem like we were going to get an answer immediately. But I was heartened by the fact that no alternative schemes were proposed.

We do need the ketamine

I knew we had enough alprazolam and atropine to ease the boys' anxiety and dry their mouths. But I told the Thai medical people, 'Assuming we are going in the morning, we do need the ketamine prepared.' I explained exactly what ketamine doses I wanted and what size syringes. In my mind, I had divided the boys into two groups: the forty-kilo kids and the fifty-kilo kids. I was basing the dosages around that. The fifty-kilo group would get 250 milligrams of ketamine to start with. The forty-kilo kids would get 200 milligrams. I knew I could vary the doses to suit the kids' more precise weights, but that would make things a whole lot more complicated for the divers. I needed to keep the process simple.

Deciding on the right top-up for intramuscular ketamine was anybody's guess. Nobody usually does it. If a patient started rousing in the operating theatre, you'd already have an IV inserted, and tiny doses would be slowly titrated in. But I needed an answer. 'Let's say a half-dose,' I declared. 'That'll be about right.' None of this is standard medical practice, because there was nothing standard about this situation.

In my entire career, I think I had given one person a dose of intramuscular ketamine, a massive psychiatric patient in an emergency department. I'd jabbed him in the leg like I was darting a dangerous animal and run away as quickly as I could, waiting for him to drop. And I'd never done an intramuscular top-up. We were making it up as we went along.

Even without formal approval, the Thai medical people got to work – just in case, I guess. All of this, from the initial dose to the top-ups, involved a little bit of science. I tried not to let on just how much guesswork was also involved.

14
HARD CHOICES
CRAIG

Our rescue plan was as solid as we could make it, whatever its limitations. Harry seemed comfortable with his makeshift operating theatre – not perfect, but good enough. I felt confident about the medical assessment I'd give each boy in chamber 8, and about the pass-off strategy we'd settled on too. Harry had promised to teach the other divers how to inject ketamine in the morning, and I figured they'd be okay. I wouldn't want them performing complex surgery, but giving injections isn't too hard. Even the sceptical Thai authorities seemed to be coming round, allowing the medical staff to count out the pills and load the syringes with ketamine. But there was one remaining question, truly a matter of life and death.

One brutal question

What would we do if the kids began to die?

It was a brutal question, but unavoidable. Heather and

Fiona had asked it before we'd even left Australia, and it had been haunting Harry and me from the moment we began to accept that anaesthesia was really the only practical option. If kids started dying, would we continue? Or would we stop and reconsider, knowing that we'd already considered every option we could think of? How many dead boys would it take until we said *no more*? One? Two? Five? How many? And if we abandoned the plan we had settled on, what alternatives did we have?

If you think these are easy questions, you haven't given them enough thought.

There were, after all, a few possible outcomes. It was unlikely but *possible* that the plan would work perfectly, and everyone would survive. Children and divers both. If that happened, the only question would be how and where to celebrate? But on the other hand, what if it didn't go so well, as we feared it might? What if the first boy died on the way out of the cave? Would we send another boy after him? What if we did, and he died too? Could we bring ourselves to keep sending more boys on that perilous underwater journey?

Harry and I needed to prepare ourselves for this very real possibility. Everyone involved in this plan fully expected that at least some of these children would die.

'I have to tell you,' Harry said to me in the DFAT van as we headed for the hotel that night, 'if the first couple die, I might have to stop. I'm not sure I'll be able to keep sending children to their deaths.'

This was difficult for Harry to say. He gets a kick out of working in the most life-threatening crises imaginable, ready to do his best no matter how dreadful the circumstances or how daunting the odds. But doctors are supposed to save people, not kill them.

'I get that,' I told him.

Harry and I would be the ones making the call, Harry especially. Depending on what happened with the first few children, he would have to decide whether or not to anaesthetise the boys who were waiting to go next.

'You know, I'm still not convinced any of this is going to work,' he said.

'Harry,' I said, when I saw the look on his face, 'we've gone round and round, and this is the best of all the possible options. We can't leave them in there for months until the monsoon season is over. If we do that, they'll surely die. If we bring them out now, there's a chance some will survive.'

Harry didn't seem convinced. 'So are you saying that at least if they die this way, they'll die asleep under the water rather than suffer a painful, lingering death in the cave that might take months? Is that it?'

'It's an impossible choice,' I conceded. 'But this part is up to you. You have to be all right with it, whatever you decide.'

We sat in silence then as the van bounced along the bumpy streets of Mae Sai, each of us lost in thought. Finally, 'I think I have to go ahead with it,' Harry said, almost in a whisper, as if he were really talking to himself. 'At least if they drown, they'll be anesthetised. When it happens, they'll be asleep. They won't know anything about it at all.'

I waited a moment, not sure how to answer. 'Look,' I said, 'if the first one or two kids die, I think we'll still have to push forwards. We can address anything that's gone wrong, but the equation won't have changed. The first one might die and then the next twelve might live. The first two might die and the next eleven might live. Unless we've got new information, there won't be any reason to change what we're doing. The kids will still be trapped there facing certain death. They deserve the best shot at survival, whatever that is.'

I can't say Harry and I really found an answer to this question. Perhaps there wasn't one. We'd been as plain as could be with each other. We had recognised and acknowledged the arguments on both sides. We would face the issue if and when we had to – but we desperately hoped we never would. Until then, it was just a horrible question hanging in the air.

It wasn't the only one, of course. There was also the question of who should be told if the children started to die during the extraction. The Thai government officials? The families? The media? The boys themselves?

'Your friends just drowned on their way out of the cave – are you ready to go now?'

I would report to Harry after the first boy arrived in chamber 8, letting him know when it was safe to send the next one, but if a boy died after leaving chamber 8, we wouldn't know until that evening. The only way to get a message through was with a cave diver – and all of them would be in the cave already, participating in the rescue. If each dive took three or four hours, we'd already have sent the next unconscious boys on their way, possibly to their deaths. It was a chilling thought.

But we would know before the second day of the rescue. What then?

Should we lie?

Should we tell the other children? Should we tell the SEALs? Or should we lie?

Despite the high value I have always placed on openness and honesty – I was inclined to lie. I would say to the remaining children, 'Everyone's okay,' even if they weren't.

I couldn't believe I was thinking like this. But telling the truth would make things drastically worse for all the remaining boys. Harry finally agreed that he might have no real option but to lie.

In a perfect world, everyone should be able to make informed choices. But how could the boys judge the best available course? We had both the experience and the knowledge, and it was up to us to make that decision for them. Sometimes, somebody just needs to take charge. This time, we would be the ones to choose, uncomfortably, on their behalf.

15
MED SCHOOL
HARRY

We heard nothing more from the Thai authorities on Saturday night. It seemed they were still deciding whether to trust the lives of thirteen young people to a scruffy band of foreigners who claimed to be experts at cave diving. Ideally, the elite Royal Thai Navy SEALs would be handling everything, not just babysitting the children.

Diplomatic immunity

By the time Craig and I headed back to our rooms, we'd heard nothing about our diplomatic immunity, either. If something went wrong in the cave, would I be held legally responsible? The decision was finally made at seven minutes to midnight: the Foreign Minister approved the granting of 'diplomatic privileges and immunities … on condition that the Thai authorities have chosen the sedation method in support of the said rescue mission'.

Michael Costa emailed us at 3.18 a.m. – did he ever sleep? – but Craig and I didn't see the email until Sunday morning. 'I will also get in writing that the Thais approved your sedation method,' Michael added in his forwarding note. *How?* I wondered. The Thais hadn't actually told us they *did* approve of our sedation method.

When Craig and I got to the Thai medical tent around 8 a.m., we still didn't know if the rescue was a goer, but all the signs were pointing to yes. Thai nurses and medics had spent the night preparing and labelling syringes – *full dose, half-dose, large boy, small boy* – just as I had asked them to, simple and clear as could be. One of the nurses showed me the drugs in a pair of large styrofoam eskies. I transferred the loaded syringes into four ziploc bags and labelled each one. Then Craig and I headed over to the Brits' headquarters to meet all the divers who'd be going into the cave with us, if and when we received formal permission. I had a first-year medical school class to teach.

Anaesthesia 101

Our best guess was that it would take a diver three or four hours to ferry one of the boys out of the cave. There was no way an initial injection of ketamine was going to last that long. Each diver would need to give a top-up dose the moment his boy seemed to be stirring. I didn't want one of the kids coming to, thrashing around and drowning himself *and* the diver who was trying to get him out.

It would be best if the unscheduled wake-up happened at one of the designated chamber stops. But it could just as easily happen underwater in one of the sumps. I needed to get all the divers comfortable enough to give these top-up shots. It would be a stretch for some of them – they were divers, not doctors – and most had never handled a syringe. Giving a jab is completely routine for a doctor or, especially, a nurse. But for someone without medical training, it can be extremely intimidating.

I'd better take this slowly, I thought.

'It all starts with you looking at the kid,' I said. 'If you think he looks like one of the smaller ones, use *this* syringe.' I held up one of the clearly labelled 100s. 'If you think he looks like one of the bigger kids, use *this* syringe.' I waved a 125.

'How many of you have given injections before?' I asked the divers.

Only Claus raised his hand. He had trained as a remote emergency medical technician and had been with the Red Cross in his native Denmark.

All the others expressed some concern. It was time to demonstrate.

I had an empty plastic water bottle and a couple of empty syringes, which I passed out to the guys. 'Okay, everyone,' I said. 'Here are some empty syringes and bungs and caps and needles. I want you to assemble one of these, pretend it's got liquid in it and inject it into this water bottle.'

Really? they seemed to ask without saying a word. I pressed on.

'I want it to go in at least three-quarters of the length of the needle, then you're going to squeeze the imaginary liquid slowly into the flesh.'

I passed the bottle to the first diver, who slid the needle through the plastic and depressed the plunger. The injection looked fairly smooth.

'Easy, eh?' I said encouragingly.

He didn't answer, just passed the bottle to the next diver, who performed his own injection and passed the bottle on. Everyone had a go. They seemed to be getting the hang of it fairly quickly. They were sliding through plastic, of course, not human tissue. Mentally, it's a different thing. But these were can-do cave divers, and they all performed better than I expected them to.

We still had to make the leap from water bottle to sedated boy, and that required further explanation.

'The best thing to do,' I said, 'is to inject the outside front quarter of the upper leg, anywhere on the outside thigh between the knee and the hip. Make sure you push the needle in far enough so that you get through the wetsuit. If you inject the drug into the wetsuit, it's not going to work. Don't worry if you go too far and hit the bone.'

There were noticeable winces.

'Just come back a little and then inject it,' I continued. 'You won't hurt the kid. You won't do any harm. There are no nerves or blood vessels there. Just bung it in and inject it. It will work. If you get it in their body, it will work – every time.'

Ketamine, I explained, is an extremely safe drug. 'Don't worry about overdosing the kid,' I said. 'Just make sure you're safe by having the kid quiet at all times. If he looks like he's rousing, give him some more. But don't give them two doses in less than about ten minutes. It takes a few minutes to work, so let the first dose take effect. Apart from that, just go for it.' I looked around to see if everyone seemed comfortable. 'Nothing can possibly go wrong,' I added earnestly.

I'm sure they saw right through my exaggerated confidence. But they also looked reassured.

'The drug,' I said, 'has its own unique effects. Patients can appear slightly strange while they are sleeping. Sometimes, they might be moaning or moving around a little. Sometimes, their eyes are open, even though the brain is still in sleep mode. On ketamine, the dividing line between asleep and awake can be a little blurry.'

Simple rule of thumb, I told the divers: 'If you're in doubt, if the child is rousing or moving to the point of it being a problem, give him more.'

Each child, I predicted, would need two or three doses on the way out.

With that, the first and only lecture in Anaesthesia 101 was over.

I passed out the first-day batches of ketamine, two or three doses for each diver. Most of the divers seemed okay. Claus seemed deeply affected by the assignment, but he didn't want to discuss it. Perhaps he was telling himself: *We have a job to do. Let's get on with it.*

Jason seemed fine to me – he was a bit like Craig: focused and driven.

I did get a quiet moment alone with John. Of all the divers, he was the only one who expressed genuine disquiet about what lay ahead. The prospect of bringing dead children out of the cave was preying on his mind.

'I hope we won't regret this,' he said.

It was just then that we got the final word. The plan had been approved by the Thai authorities.

IV
SAVING

16

FINAL PREP

HARRY

It was near 10 a.m. as we started suiting up and assembling our gear. There were too many of us to dive into the cave at once, so we split into pairs. I dived with Jason – focused, driven, unstoppable Jason – and we went in first. We had to travel farthest, all the way to chamber 9. Craig and Rick followed, and then came the others.

I was sure Pak and the SEALs would have followed all our instructions and readied the first wave of boys for their long, gruelling, sedated trips out. Fasted them. Dressed them. Prepared them mentally. Confirmed which ones would be up first. And had boy number one shipshape and ready to go.

Jason is such a machine in the water, I was happy I could keep up with him. But why did I feel so spent?

Weak as a kitten

This was the main event. Twelve Thai children and their young soccer coach were waiting expectantly, desperately hoping we could save their lives. The whole world was tuned in. I needed to be at my absolute best. But by the time Jason and I were halfway to chamber 9, I felt cold and shivery – weak as a kitten – as if I was getting the flu.

I really can't afford to blow this, I said to myself.

I had a diving pouch clipped off behind me like a little purse containing all the drugs, syringes and needles. Craig, Rick and the others, diving in behind us, would stash their ketamine top-ups in a wetsuit pocket, or waterproof bags. Along with their supply of drugs, Rick, Jason, John and Chris would each swim into the cave with an extra cylinder and a full face mask for the boys to use. Those cylinders contained 80 per cent oxygen, a higher percentage than usual, though not the pure oxygen we had hoped to use.

Some patients breathe inadequately under anaesthesia. In a normal operating theatre, increased oxygen helps keep patients nice and pink. But there was a more important reason this time: if your body is primed with oxygen, your brain will live longer after your breathing stops. On a high-risk dive like this one, that could mean the difference between brain damage, life and death. With sufficient oxygen and in a slightly cooled, anaesthetised patient, the brain might survive as long as ten minutes, twice the normal time.

I hoped we'd never need that extra margin of safety, but we'd sure be grateful to have it if we did. Unfortunately, the Thai Navy personnel who were filling the oxygen cylinders had somehow managed to destroy all the booster pumps so we couldn't fill the tanks to sufficient pressure with pure oxygen. A bit more than three-quarters full was as high as we could go. So we topped off the boys' cylinders with regular air to create sufficient pressure.

I was feeling lightheaded and a little nauseated as Jason and I swam into chamber 8. We lingered there as Craig and Rick arrived. 'It's almost like the gas I've been breathing isn't clean,' I said to the others. But Jason looked okay. So did Craig and Rick. At least so far. But we had work to do. All we could do was swim on.

The boys had an excellent view from atop their ledge and noticed us before we noticed them. They seemed even more hyped than they had the day before. As we approached, I could hear their chattering voices. This was a big day for us. It was so much bigger for them. If any of the boys felt nervous about the death-defying journey ahead, I didn't sense it in the chamber's dank air. It felt like we'd just swum into Christmas morning, and I was Santa Claus.

The first boys

Jason and I took our gear off and laid it on the small beach across the water from the hill where the boys were. Then we swam over to the base of the slope with the cylinder, the full face mask and the pouch filled with drugs, needles and syringes. I found the rope over to the right, where I clipped my little goodie bag so it would stay out of the unsanitary water.

Dr Pak came down the mud slide far more steadily than Craig or I had the day before. I was beginning to realise that Dr Pak always looked in command. I thought: he probably wakes up every morning cleanshaven and wearing a perfectly pressed uniform shirt.

'G'day,' I called. 'How are you? Have you got the kids ready?'

'They're ready,' he said. 'Six of them. I fasted them from zero-six-hundred like you asked.'

That's when I had to deliver the day's first bit of bad news. 'Unfortunately, we've only got four full face masks that will fit the boys. So only four will be going today.'

Nobody complained about the late change, and I couldn't tell if any of them were relieved or disappointed. Someone had to decide which four of the six were still set to go. How'd you like to make that call? It would be up to Dr Pak, Coach Ekk and the boys themselves.

From the bottom of the hill, I could see that some of the boys had already pulled on the wetsuits that the British divers had brought in over the previous few days. Were they itching to go – or what? I gave Dr Pak a strip of alprazolam tabs that I fetched from the goodie bag. 'You might as well hang on to these,' I said to him. 'I want each kid to take one tablet when I call for him. Don't give it until I say so.'

It was such a relief to have a real medical pro looking after the boys. When Dr Pak said he would take care of something, I had no doubt that he would. 'So go ahead and give the first kid a tablet,' I said. Dr Pak nodded, then headed back up the slippery slope to the boys. Jason was right on his heels.

Note

The first boy was one of the taller ones. His name was Prachak Sutham, but his friends all called him Note. He'd turned fifteen exactly one week earlier, the eighth day the boys were trapped in the cave. An easygoing eighth-grader at Mae Sai Prasitsart School, the same one attended by Tern, Night, Mick and Dom, Note was known as a bright, quiet boy. He had a two-year-old sister and a father who worked in a local auto-repair shop, where Note helped out on weekends. 'When you teach him how to fix something in the garage,' one of the father's co-workers told CNN, 'he'll learn how to do it after just one go.' Note was one of the stronger players on the Wild Boars soccer team, and an ardent fan of the Thai Premier League's Chiang Rai United. But neither Jason nor I knew any of that as he began to prepare Note for his risky underwater trip. All we knew was that this boy was the first one, and it was Jason's daunting responsibility to get him out alive.

As the lean, dark-haired boy stood silently in front of him, Jason made sure the wetsuit fitted snugly. He adjusted the diving hood and then the buoyancy device that went over the boy's head like a life jacket, double-checking the oral inflator and the string that's supposed to dump the air with a single, stiff pull. This device could keep a diver – even an unconscious one, we hoped – neutral in the water, preventing him from floating too high or sinking too low. While Jason performed each check and manoeuvre, the three Thai Navy SEALs stared intently, trying to learn the pre-dive routine so they might repeat it with future boys. That could speed future rescues, assuming there were any.

Jason wrapped a bungee around Note's chest and a second one around the boy's waist. He wrapped a cable tie around each of the boy's wrists and a second tie through each of those to make a little loop.

'It's to stop water from going into your wetsuit,' Jason told the boy, half in English, half in pantomime. That was true as far as it went. What Jason didn't mention was the other, more important reason for the cable ties: to secure the boy's hands behind his back just before the dive, when the cable ties would be clipped together with a spring-loaded metal carabiner. Some ignorant critics in the international media would later condemn this, claiming innocent children had been handcuffed like hardened prisoners. Securing the boys' hands was an important safety measure, protecting their extremities from being twisted, banged or mangled along the way. It would also ensure that if a boy did wake up unexpectedly, he wouldn't rip off his face mask and drown. For a similar reason, the boys' feet would also be bound before their long dives out. When people panic underwater, even small boys, they can have great strength and be extremely dangerous to themselves and their rescuers.

We wanted sleek, compact, human packages, gliding through the water.

Thinking of them as packages helped us to dissociate ourselves from the fact that these were indeed living, breathing young humans whom we could easily be sending to their deaths. Much as we cared about these children, we had a job to do that required technical proficiency and a certain emotional distance. That was always a struggle for me.

Field hospital

As Jason continued with his dive-prep routine at the boys' elevated camp site, I was readying my own makeshift anaesthetic room at the bottom of the slope. I chose the spot carefully. I wanted a flat, stable, water's-edge location where I could lay out what I'd need, have room to work and, just as important, get a small measure of privacy for myself and the boy.

What I settled on was far from ideal. I'd be standing waist-deep in the turbid water at the base of the slope, my drugs balanced precariously on the open pouch I had suspended from the nearby line. I'd have none of the equipment or personnel I was used to in hospital, even the raggedy ones in far-off places I'd worked in over the years. Here, there was no electricity or light, other than the one on my caving helmet. No surgeons, techs or nurses, or even a squirt bottle of hand sanitiser or a clean strip of gauze. I was in the remotest of locations performing the most rudimentary field medicine under the direst conditions at the mercy of the latest weather report. It was just my young patient, my syringes, my drugs, my wits and me – and some of the best cave divers on the planet.

'We're going to take you down to Dr Harry now,' Jason said, once the boy was finally outfitted and the alprazolam was beginning to take a grip. The anti-anxiety tablet,

I hoped, would quell any last-minute jitters. It would also – and I hadn't thought enough about this part – make the kid a little woozy.

As I looked up and saw the groggy boy wobbling down the muddy slope, I did briefly wonder: *Should I have waited for the kid to climb down before I drugged him?*

Too late now.

17

FIRST BOY

HARRY

Ready, steady – *come on down.*

As Note wobbled down the slope in his wetsuit, buoyancy collar and hood, I was waiting impatiently at the bottom of the hill, up to my waist in water. Jason was one step behind him, but I was still holding my hands out, ready to catch the boy if he lost his footing and came crashing down.

Maybe it was the adrenaline of the moment or my relief that we were finally getting started, or maybe I'd just had time to catch my breath after the long dive in, but I was starting to feel a little better. Not great, but better. I wasn't quite as convinced I was getting the flu.

As the boy reached the bottom, Jason at his side, Pak was only a couple of steps behind. I was already getting myself into position, half in the dirt beside the hill, half in the coffee-coloured water below. We were really going to do this.

I knelt on my left leg, pushing my knee into the mud, and sat the kid on my right thigh. It was an awkward position, but I needed to lean into the mud to stop myself from sliding any further into the water. Once I got the boy to sit there, I started talking to him. Babbling, really. 'What's your name?' 'How old are you?'

At the same time, I was patting the boy on the shoulder and steadying him on my knee.

'Good boy, good boy,' I said. 'What position do you play on the soccer team? My name's Harry. I'm a doctor. We're going to get you out of here. Are you ready to go home yet? Or would you prefer to hang out in the cave a little longer?'

Since the boy spoke so little English, roughly equivalent to the amount of Thai I know, I didn't get too many answers during our get-to-know-you interview. He did mention that his name was Note. But the point of all that chatter was for me to calm and distract him. That's one of the things anaesthetists do, along with sending the patients off and making sure they come back alive. We fill the air and ease the nerves. Who knew if I distracted young Note? Did he notice that I was about to jab a needle into his thigh – and then a second one?

In the operating theatre, I like to have the little ones sitting on their mum's lap. I'll come in close and touch them and talk rubbish so it all seems routine. I turned to Pak, inviting him into our little chat. 'Tell him I'm Dr Harry, and I'm a famous soccer player myself.'

Pak shot me a conspiratorial smile and pressed ahead. I could tell everyone was trying to make a bit of a joke of it. It was all gelling. Pak is such an upbeat, optimistic guy, it's hard to feel like there's any danger when he's around, the legendary Thai hero.

Ready for the injection?

Then, without making a big deal of it, I put my left hand on Note's leg and held up the syringe with my right. I blurted out a quick: 'Ready for the injection?'

'Oh, okay,' the boy nodded.

I squeezed a shot of atropine through the thin rubber of his wetsuit and into his leg, feeling each layer of resistance as I went. Rubber. Skin. Muscle. I had done this often enough to stop before I hit bone.

I could see him screw up his eyes a little. There was a bit of a sting. Then I pulled out the needle and rubbed his leg and said in the most compelling tone I had: 'Well done. Good work.'

I leaned over and stuck the syringe into the mud so the needle would be safe for now.

I watched the boy for a second; he looked totally fine. He wasn't crying or breathing hard or seeming the least bit jumpy. His attitude was more like, *I've had shots before. That wasn't so bad. I'm brave.*

Then, I pulled out the second syringe, the ketamine.

'There will be a second one,' I said, as matter-of-factly as I could.

Again, no alarm. No drama. Routine as could be.

I gave the other leg a quick rub. 'Here comes the ketamine.'

Needle in, no problem, no yelp, no tears.

In addition to a slight facial scrunch-up, I got something else from Note as the ketamine began spreading out from the large muscle at the front of his thigh. He gave me the slightest little thankyou bow as he faded towards unconsciousness.

Which I found totally endearing.

What else do you need to know about the gentleness of the Thai people?

Jason was standing near us at the bottom of the hill, holding a full face mask ready for the boy. He tested it a couple more times, holding it up against his own face to make sure it was breathing all right. So far, so good. At the same time, I was holding the fading boy as securely as I could – left hand on the back of his head, right hand supporting his jaw, keeping the airway open until I was sure he was completely unconscious.

Five minutes was all that took. 'Right-o, Jason.'

With that, Jason came to stand in front of Note and me and placed the mask against the boy's placid face, covering everything from just north of his little eyebrows to a spot south of his chin. I held the mask in place while Jason pulled the straps around the back and tightened them as much as possible, then checked that no part of the diving hood had slipped inside the mask, to minimise any risk of leakage. Next step: making sure the kid was still breathing now that the mask was on, which wasn't a given at all.

There's a natural diving reflex I was concerned about, especially with inexperienced divers, even more especially with children: cold things on your face can make you hold your breath. It's a well-known phenomenon. This can last for fifteen or twenty seconds, sometimes even longer. At that point, the person will start gasping for air. So the suspended breathing isn't usually fatal or even all that dangerous. But it's a rocky way to start such a long and dangerous cave dive.

Note was breathing fine.

At this point, Jason and I leaned the boy backwards, his feet in the water, his head still out. Jason slid the air cylinder beneath the two bungees, the chest bungee snapping around the cylinder neck, the waist bungee securing the lower part of the tank. He dropped a three- or four-pound weight into the pocket on the front of the buoyancy device. Then, I performed my first pre-dive test, which tested me as much as it tested the boy.

Rolling Note over, I pushed his face into the water and held it there. It felt so wrong, shoving the face of an unconscious child underwater and holding it there. It felt too close to drowning a child. But I needed to see if he was still breathing steadily through the mask even as his mouth and nose were fully submerged. Were bubbles floating to the surface of the water? Bubbles equal breathing equals life.

There were bubbles. I could see them, being exhaled in strong bursts in the harsh, white beam of my helmet light. Note was breathing well, and water did not appear to be leaking into the mask. When I lifted his head out of the water, the inside of the mask looked dry.

This, all by itself, was a monumental accomplishment. A sedated child was breathing underwater, completely unconscious, inhaling and exhaling full breaths of air. In the history of scuba, in the history of anaesthesia, in the history of children, I'm not sure this had ever been attempted before, much less achieved.

At this point, Jason went off to collect his own dive gear, which he'd left on the beach across the water at the far side of chamber 9. He suited up for the arduous, multi-hour journey out, above and below the waterline. It would be a dive like no other ever attempted, accompanied by an unconscious fifteen-year-old. Again, I pushed the boy face down in the water, let him breathe there, then sat him up again, making sure the head straps were tight enough and no water had snuck into the mask. I did that a couple of times. Dry as a bone. I cinched the mask straps up one more time to be sure.

When Jason returned, he took a few minutes to test his own equipment, then helped me with Note's final prep list. Quickly, I glanced up the hill, but no curious little eyes were watching. With Note still face down in the water, we pulled his hands behind his back, restraining them with the wrist-tie cable loops and the spring-loaded carabiner. The symbolism of that also seemed terrible to me. However pure our intentions, we were handcuffing this child. Then Jason used another bungee to bind the boy's ankles loosely together. All of it was disquieting but necessary. As we had learned so vividly from our own dives in and out, some of the openings in this cave were ridiculously narrow. Note's trim body had to be as compact and contained as possible. We couldn't risk him getting snagged on anything along the way.

With that, they were almost ready to go.

Jason had two ways of holding onto young Note in the water and guiding him along. There was a small handle on the back of the boy's buoyancy device that Jason could grip onto, either swimming side by side or gliding along the surface with the boy an easy arm's length below. Jason also clipped a one-metre length of rope to Note's back. If the British diver chose to, he could clip the other end of the rope to his own harness. That way, he wouldn't risk dropping the line and letting the child float away, even if his own hands got busy doing something else. That could be potentially deadly.

'You ready?' I asked Jason.

He nodded. Jason was always ready.

Go

The drugs had done what they were supposed to. So had Pak. So had I. The boy was fully sedated and all suited up. His mask wasn't leaking. His underwater breathing was strong. Neither Jason nor I had any idea how long any of that would continue to be true. But all the signs said, *Go.*

As Jason waded deeper into the water, with the boy floating beside him, I lingered at the bottom of the hill with Pak just above me. We stood silently for a moment, knowing exactly how much was at stake here, neither one of us saying a word.

By then, the British diver was towing the Thai boy down the tunnel, only the back of Jason's wetsuit visible from where we were.

That's when I turned to Pak and said: 'Next kid. Next tablet.'

What was I thinking? I was supposed to wait for Jason and his boy to reach chamber 8, where Rick, Mikko, Claus and Craig could check on the boy. Then, Rick would swim back to me with our very first progress report: had boy number one survived the first leg of the high-risk journey? Were we killing these children or saving them? What was working flawlessly? What should we avoid at all cost?

I'm not sure why I was in such a hurry. But with the first boy so painlessly on his way – *not a single tear* – all my instincts told me: get on with boy number two. I had completely forgotten an important part of the plan.

Tern

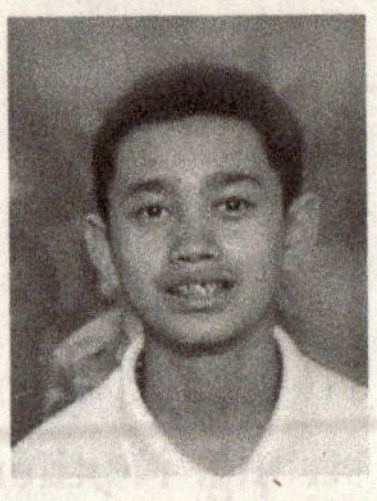

Number two turned out to be fourteen-year-old Natthawut Thakhamsai – Tern to his friends. Another eighth-grader at Mae Sai Prasitsart School, Tern was a Wild Boars defender. But he was beloved as the team's unofficial comedian, able to make everyone erupt in laughter with his goofy faces, his hilarious jokes and his wicked mimicry. With his twinkly eyes and gap-toothed grin, it was almost impossible not to like Tern, his friends all agreed. And now, if things kept going smoothly, he'd really have something to smile about.

Pak and I were joined at the chamber 9 beach by John Volanthen and Chris Jewell, two of Rick Stanton's other aces. John was up next. It would be his responsibility to ferry young Tern out of the cave. They were a good match. John had got his own start in caves as a fourteen-year-old Scout. Now, he'd be taking a fourteen-year-old on his very first cave dive, a trip that just might save the boy's life. But John was even quieter than usual, the gravity of the situation weighing heavily on him.

With his help and Pak's, I repeated the same drill on Tern that Jason and I had performed on Note. Anti-anxiety tablet. Wobbly stumble down the slippery slope to the water. Soothing chit-chat on my knee. Atropine in one leg, ketamine in the other. A five-minute slide into dreamland. Suited up. Faced down. Underwater breathing tests. Tied up like a parcel at Australia Post. And off they swam, John with one hand on the guide rope, one hand on Tern's back handle, down the chamber 9 tunnel towards Craig and the divers I could only assume were waiting in chamber 8. Boy number two was on his way.

My first official screw-up

By racing ahead prematurely, I hadn't left much room between the first two teams. I certainly didn't want to start the rescue mission with a blind, muddy-water traffic jam. I could only hope that, with a little luck, the second team didn't bang into the first team from behind. And what if Rick was on his way to chamber 9 and crashed into John and Tern in a narrow part of the cave? There was now the risk of a rear-ender, *and* a head-on collision.

Yes, this was my first official screw-up.

I was suddenly feeling nervous. Where the hell was Rick? I had already sent two boys into the murky abyss. What horrible fate had befallen them? Maybe in some eruption of panic and raw strength, they had already dragged their own rescuers down with them. With the added burden of knowing I had sent the second boy sooner than I should have, failing to wait for Rick's progress report, I felt alone with my thoughts. If only I knew what was happening in chamber 8.

The mind has an extraordinary capacity for creating lurid scenarios.

18
CHAMBER

CRAIG

The tiniest vibration – that's all it was at first. I had my fingers on the line, waiting for some barely perceptible rope movement to alert me that someone was coming towards us and we'd better get ready for a burst of activity.

How long had Rick and I been waiting in chamber 8? An hour? Longer? It's about a 300-metre dive through the sump from chamber 9 to chamber 8. Figure on twenty minutes for an experienced diver alone, obviously a bit longer for escorting a sedated boy, especially the first one.

I couldn't see anything yet. The water was murky. Helmet lights are never bright enough. Rick and I were on the beach at the edge of the water, peering out towards chamber 9.

Mikko and Claus

Where were Mikko and Claus, the two European divers who

were supposed to help us get the boy across the dry terrain of chamber 8?

Mikko Paasi and Claus Rasmussen were tough, experienced divers. Claus, the Dane with medical and injection experience, had worked with refugees and asylum seekers before moving to Thailand and joining Ben Reymenants' dive business. His talent for languages – he seemed fluent in Thai – would come in handy communicating with the boys. Harry and I had just met Mikko, though we wouldn't soon forget him, not with his shoulder-length dreadlocks, his driven attitude and his weightlifter's physique. A native of Finland, Mikko is the founder of a diving centre on the small Thai island of Koh Tao, where he specialises in ocean and wreck diving. These were not no-show guys.

Whatever the explanation, it wasn't just the Europeans' extra hands we needed once Jason and Note arrived. We also wanted the sked they were bringing with them.

A sked is a compact rescue stretcher designed for confined spaces, a flat piece of tough plastic that rolls up into the size of a big sleeping-bag. These skeds are amazingly rugged. You can drag them. You can move them through the water fairly easily. You can strap the patient in and transport him across almost anything. The sked protects against injury, and it's easy to use. It would be perfect, we figured, for dragging sedated boys across what everyone expected would be an especially gnarly dry section of the cave. But since Mikko and Claus hadn't turned up yet, neither had their green sked.

Fairly quickly after the rope began to move, a glow

appeared in the brown sump water between chamber 8 and chamber 9, dim at first, then gradually brighter. Then bubbles began to appear and a diver's helmet popped out of the water. It was Jason.

Still breathing

He stopped at the point where the beach goes down into the water and knelt there for a second, organising himself, then flashed a tight smile at Rick and me and passed the boy up the beach as far as he could push. Jason was in dive gear, so he wouldn't be much use on land. Rick and I were just in our wetsuits, much freer to move.

I didn't know which boy it was, but over time I would learn to tell the difference between the big ones and small ones. For now, though, I just knew that without the sked, he was going to be heavy, whoever he was. He was still a patient, someone who needed to be examined, perhaps consoled, maybe sedated again and sent on his way as quickly and efficiently as possible. This was a complex operation, and we were a vital part of it.

As gently as we could, Rick and I pulled his body onto the beach, his head and chest on the sand, his feet still dangling in the water. We rolled him onto his side, which made it easier to get the cylinder off his chest, then rolled him the rest of the way onto his back, face up. I took his full face mask off and got my first good look at his face.

'He's still breathing,' Jason said.

We waited for Jason to say something else, but I guess that was his main focus and his main worry. I put my fingers up to the boy's mouth. The breath felt steady and strong. Then, I continued with what I would call a rudimentary veterinary field examination.

I pulled his lip up and looked at the colour of his gums; they were nice and pink – not blue.

I pressed on the gum until it turned white, then released my finger. The gum should turn pink again in one second, definitely no longer than two. That tells us how well the patient's blood is flowing to the peripheral parts of his body. The white disappeared fast. From that I knew his heart was beating well and his blood flow was strong.

I felt inside his mouth to see if he was warm. His temperature was fine, which I expected. He hadn't been in the water all that long. While I was focused on the boy's mouth, I also made sure he hadn't vomited and that he wasn't producing a lot of saliva. Things seemed fairly dry in there. None of this was a hospital-level examination. In fact, doctors reading this are probably shaking their heads, aghast. But a good basic once-over was the best I could do in the circumstances, and he seemed fine. All along, I was looking for signs that the boy might be waking from his anaesthetic slumber. Were his hands moving? Were his feet? I checked his palpebral reflex, tapping in the corner of his eye to see if the eyelid moved. That's a very early sign of lightening anaesthetic. His eyelid twitched vigorously as I tapped there.

He wasn't wide awake. Not even close. But his sleep was definitely lighter than was ideal. 'We need to top him up,' I said to Rick, who readily agreed.

I reached into my kit and removed one of the syringes so I could administer a half-dose of ketamine, a drug I'd given to countless dogs and other animals over the years, though Note would be my first drowsy boy. Ketamine is used far less routinely with humans than with animals. I know how they respond to it. I know what they look like when they're waking up. I can tell how much more is needed. All those responses, I reasoned, should be similar with these boys, who weren't any larger than some of the big dogs I had treated and definitely smaller than the horses and kangaroos. I would never claim to have anywhere near the expertise that Harry has as an anaesthetic specialist, far from it. But generally speaking, in veterinary surgery, one person is both the surgeon and the anaesthetist. So I'd sedated patients thousands of times.

I poked the needle through the thin wetsuit and into the boy's thigh. I gave the syringe a gentle squeeze. Soon, I could see his sleep deepen. That part was easy. What came next was hard.

Hard and clumsy

Jason was still in most of his dive gear, so he wasn't much good to us on land. Claus, Mikko and their sked still hadn't arrived. That left Rick and me to lug the clumsy weight of a sleeping boy across the long dry section of chamber 8.

We grabbed him under his arms while also supporting his head, Rick on the left, me on the right, our grips wrapped from armpit to shoulder. His feet more or less dragged behind. It wasn't the smoothest form of locomotion or the easiest, but each step got us closer to the water at the other side of the chamber, where Jason could resume the long dive out.

We didn't mind dragging the boy's feet on the sandy beach or in the shallow water along the way. But when we got to the rocky section further along, then we had to carry him. For that stretch, I held the boy's ankles, and Rick had the underarm grip. It was difficult. Note wasn't particularly big or heavy, But if you've ever tried to carry a limp person any distance at all, you'll know how hard and clumsy it can be.

Jason didn't waste any time. He was busy too. He moved all his own gear across the dry part of the chamber and then walked back and got the kid's cylinder, mask and vest.

We had to get through a bit of a duck. It was only a couple of metres long, but there was water to wade across, and at one stage it was chest-deep. Then it was neck deep. But we could always touch the bottom, and we held firmly onto Note, keeping his head above water. This was definitely a walk, not a dive, and we just kept plodding onwards, not fast, but steady. There was another duck at the far end, the demarcation between chamber 8 and chamber 7. Later in the rescue, as the water dropped, the two chambers would become a single chamber with no sump and no duck between them, just an imaginary line.

Jason had all the dive gear waiting there for us, both his and Note's. When we arrived, he was getting himself ready to climb back into the water.

Something wrong with the air

I asked Jason how he was doing.

'The diving's okay,' he said. 'But I'm not feeling right in the water. There might be something wrong with the air we're breathing.'

Come to think of it, I wasn't feeling so hot myself. I'd had a headache on the dive in, which is rare for me. None of us had been drinking the night before, and I was well hydrated. The air in the tanks was the obvious explanation. Rick piped up and said the air smelled bad to him. We would have to check the compressor that was being used to fill the tanks. But for now, we would just have to proceed, bad air or not. Luckily, the boys were breathing 80 per cent oxygen with only a small amount of air in their cylinders, so they shouldn't be affected.

Rick and I began getting the boy shipshape to dive again. We were definitely learning our procedures on this first transfer and check-up, but I was confident we'd improve as more boys came through and we practised our moves.

I checked the boy's sedation level one last time. He seemed fully out to me. We wished them luck and sent them on their way.

Rick knew that Harry was waiting in chamber 9 to hear his early report – or, as it would turn out, *not* waiting but still needing to hear it. Rick was also supposed to dive boy number four out of the cave. But with still no sign of Mikko and Claus, he didn't want to leave me alone in chamber 8. Would I need him to help carry the next boy across? But was

Harry waiting for Rick before sending another boy through?

We didn't have to wait long to find out.

Boy number two

The rope began moving again. The lights appeared in the water. It was quicker than either of us expected, but here was boy number two and his able British dive escort, John Volanthen.

'His name is Tern,' John said to Rick and me after emerging from the water. 'Have a look, but he seems to be doing okay.'

I was happy to hear that. I was also happy to notice that the second boy seemed a little smaller – and a little lighter, I hoped – than the first one. Luckily, things were going well so far.

We pulled young Tern out of the water and stripped off the heavy parts of his gear. John took off some of his own. Like Jason before him, he would lug the boy's equipment and then his own to the far side of the chamber.

I could tell right away that Tern would also need a ketamine top-up. Breathing, temperature, blood flow were all fine, but he was definitely twitchy in his sedation. This was already becoming a pattern. One dose was not going to be enough, not for a nine-chamber dive as long and complex as this one. I gave Tern the shot before Rick and I began carrying him across the sand and just about to the rocky section. Then, without a word of warning, Claus and Mikko appeared.

Apparently, they had thought they were supposed to be at a different location. Never having dived this far into the cave, they weren't exactly sure of the layout. They wanted to hear how things had been going and were eager to help. But: 'Where's the sked?' I demanded.

The stretcher, for some reason, was back at the near side of chamber 7.

'Well, go and get it,' I snapped. 'We need it.'

Rick was eager to head to chamber 9 to report to Harry. He needed to get his own boy. But he stayed with me and Tern while Claus and Mikko went off to fetch the stretcher. When they got back, we had carried Tern most of the way across the chamber anyway.

Despite the rocky start, Mikko and Claus would prove to be hugely valuable partners as the mission rolled on. Claus could handle just about anything. Mikko was strong as a bull, able to drag that sked across any imaginable terrain, with minimal assistance from anyone. Half the time I was running just to keep up with him.

19

NIGHT MOVES

HARRY

'It's all good, Harry,' Rick said once he'd climbed out of the water and sat next to me on the little beach at chamber 9.

You can imagine how relieved I was to hear that.

'The first two kids have come through,' Rick went on. 'They seem fine. They're breathing. They're asleep. Good work. Carry on.' I let out a huge sigh. I'd been more anxious than I had realised. My pounding heart needed time to slow down. Sending these boys off in decent shape was nice. Hearing that they'd made it through their first check-up was way, way better.

I was also feeling close to normal now, and I was certain that it had to be bad gas in my cylinder. We would have to check on the gas-filling operations at the end of the day.

It was much too soon to get cocky. We still had eleven rescues to go. But it's fair to say I liked the way this was going. We were on a little roll.

The boys were easily sedated. The divers were getting

them out, at least a few hundred metres into the next chamber. His report could hardly have been more encouraging.

But I still had no idea how the first boys would fare once they moved beyond chamber 8. I was fully aware of the many perils that lay ahead of them. The boys could awaken in an underwater section where giving a top-up would be almost impossible. In tight areas with no visibility, they faced the constant danger of banging their heads against the rock. I knew the divers would try to protect the boys' heads against the stalactites and unpredictable ceiling drops, allowing their own heads to take a bit of a beating. But what if a boy's torso got jammed in one of the many tiny openings? What if the passage was too narrow for him, his escort and their tanks? What if the boy's mask became dislodged? There are many ways to drown inside a flooded cave. But I couldn't distract myself with a thousand scenarios. I had to stay focused on my responsibilities, anaesthetising number three and then number four and getting them on their way, with adequate space between them this time.

I had learned that lesson, right?

Nick

Chris Jewell would be ferrying boy number three, Pipat Bodhi, once the ketamine and I did our thing. His friends all called him Nick, and he'd had his fifteenth birthday the day before the Wild Boars went into the cave. A student at Ban San Sai School, he wasn't even a member of the team. But he'd tagged along to practice that day with his friend, goalie Ekkarat 'Biw' Wongsookchan.

When the boys headed off to the cave after practice, Nick happily came too. A bright boy who sometimes struck new acquaintances as stiff and serious, his extroverted, witty side would appear as soon as he felt comfortable, as would his passion for Mookata Thai barbecue.

I didn't get to see any of that. By the time Pak gave the boy the anti-anxiety tablet and Chris got him suited up and the two of them pointed him down the slope, Nick wasn't saying much of anything. He was gentle and utterly compliant when he settled on my knee. We engaged in the usual blather. I gave him the usual shots. He responded with the quiet bravery I was getting used to. Barely any wincing at all.

Rick stood by, seeing for the first time how we did things in the farthest chamber. Chris pulled on the rest of his own gear and swam back to where I sat with an anaesthetised Nick. Chris Jewell was exactly the sort of bloke I wanted on this mission. At thirty-five, he was the youngest of the Brits, smart and strong.

And off they went, Chris and Nick, towards chamber 8 and, we could only hope, towards the friends and family and worldwide audience that had been so desperately cheering for the boys' safe release from the cave. Another one on his way to freedom.

Night

I gave the pair what I believed was plenty of lead time before moving on to the fourth boy, the last for the day, the one Rick Stanton was going to ferry out, Pheeraphat Sompiengjai. With Rick in the water, I had no doubt the boy would be in excellent hands. Known to his friends and family as Night, young Pheeraphat was another June birthday. Since he turned sixteen the day the group went missing, 23 June, he was the oldest player on the soccer team. A student at Mae Sai Prasitsart and a Wild Boars right-winger, Night was unfairly blamed by some people for the fact that the children got stuck in Tham Luang cave. While it was true that the boys went to the cave in part to celebrate Night's birthday, most of them, like many local children around Mae Sai, had been inside the cave plenty of times. They were happy to have any excuse.

Night's sister was born during the Water Festival, so their father started calling her Nam, water in Thai. Pheeraphat was born after dark. So he became Night. Night was especially close to his parents. Fifteen days earlier, Night's mother, Supaluk, had urged him to hurry home from practice. She had a SpongeBob SquarePants cake waiting for him. Now, Night's mother and father, joined by other relatives, were spending every night sleeping at the cave site.

When Night came down the slope, I recognised that he was one of the boys who seemed to have some chest congestion. I could hear it in his breathing. When I began to talk with him, there was a raspy tone in his voice. He didn't sound seriously ill to me, but there was definitely something going on.

The send-off was normal enough. We followed the same drill we had with the first three boys. Despite or perhaps because of whatever infection he was fighting, Night faded soon after he got the ketamine, quickly enough to make me nervous I had given him too much. Rick and I packaged him up according to the recipe. Then, Rick swam off with Night, back towards Mikko, Claus and Craig in chamber 8.

Rick and Night hadn't even made it out of the chamber 9 canal when Rick turned around and called out to me.

'Harry,' he yelled, 'this kid is really not breathing much.'

Rick knew the difference. He'd worked with Craig on the first two boys, whose breathing was perfectly robust. Rick's alarm was concerning, but the truth is, there wasn't much either of us could do about it, much as we would like to – not in the middle of the water.

'If you bring him back here, what am I going to do?' I yelled back. 'Just go, mate.'

I knew we had some science on our side. With 80 per cent oxygen in the tank, the boy should need only the three breaths a minute that Rick was counting. It's not ideal, but that rate of breathing will sustain life. He'd be okay. As long as his airway was open and he was getting those three proper breaths of 80 per cent oxygen, he'd be fine.

Rick swam on.

I threw on my dive gear as quickly as I could. Despite all the cheery self-talk – *three breaths a minute, 80 per cent oxygen, nothing to worry about* – I was seriously worried. I figured I'd better follow Rick and the slow-breathing boy. 'I'll see you guys tomorrow,' I called out to Pak, but with the constant threat of rain, there was no way to know if I would. I grabbed hold of the guide rope and moved towards chamber 8 as quickly as my arm pulls and fin kicks could safely carry me.

Now, it was my turn to follow the route the divers and boys were on. Visibility was absolute zero, due to the silt kicked up by the divers and the four human packages they were shepherding out of the cave. I didn't even bother keeping my eyes open.

Travelling so methodically, I wasn't sure exactly how long it would take to reach chamber 8. There was a line trap on the right where the rope pulled tight into an unpassable crevice which had to be avoided. There was a flattener where my chest and belly barely scraped through, made slightly easier by the cave's soft clay floor. Then, all of a sudden, I felt something with my right hand, something I didn't recognise.

What was that?

It felt rubbery and cold, and it was down in the mud at the floor of the cave. If I had been diving in the ocean, I'd have thought it was a fish. But whatever I touched wasn't wiggling, and there weren't any fish that I knew of in Tham Luang cave.

It took another second before it hit me. *That's a foot, a small, human foot.* It didn't seem to be moving at all.

He's not right

I still couldn't see anything, but after another second or so, I realised there was a boy attached to the foot, and Rick was attached to the boy.

As if Rick didn't have enough to deal with already: zero visibility, his kid's chest infection, the exhaustion all of us felt at the end of the day. Now, I was rear-ending him. Then my head popped above the surface just in time to see Rick pulling the boy out of the water and onto the sand. I yanked my helmet and mask off and spat out my mouthpiece, just as Craig appeared as well. Both of them looked genuinely worried.

'Is everything okay?' I asked.

'I don't think so,' Rick said, glancing down at the boy. 'He's not right. The breathing – I'm not happy with that at all.'

I quickly pulled off the rest of my gear. 'Let's pull him right up on the sand,' I said.

My heart was pumping hard now. This felt very serious to me. As far as I knew, the first boys were out without major incident. At least, they were safely on their way. Was boy number four going to be our moment of truth?

Once Night was fully on the sand, Craig and I rolled him onto his right side. He felt cold. Too cold. He didn't seem to be breathing at all.

I lay on the sand behind him. At first, I wasn't eager to remove his full face mask or cylinder. Why disrupt whatever benefits he was getting from the 80 per cent oxygen? But I needed to get his breathing going again. When I did slide off the mask, his lips looked blue. My first thought was that he might have been overdosed with anaesthetic or become hypothermic. I had also seen reactions like this before when anaesthetised children had a chest infection. They often play up under anaesthetic: their airways are irritable, they hold their breath, or get something called laryngeal spasm. It's not their fault. I reached around and lifted Night's chin then slipped my fingers into the front of his mouth, pulling his jaw forwards. That's a standard anaesthetic manoeuvre, a good way to ensure a patient's airway is open and to feel how strong the breathing is. Holding my hand in front of his mouth like that, I waited to feel the boy's warm breath on my palm.

I was totally still, instinctively holding my own breath, eager for the slightest indication. I might have felt a little something but not enough to convince myself that he was exhaling anything. If I'd held a mirror up, I don't think it would have fogged at all.

Then, I placed my hand against the boy's belly, which is another way of checking for respiratory effort. I felt some movement, but again it wasn't remotely regular or strong. A short, occasional breath – that's all I could feel. This kid was really struggling.

I stared at his face. His skin had a blueish tint. Was he blue because he wasn't breathing or blue because he was cold? I couldn't tell. *He's definitely not breathing enough. I'm going to have to roll him over for mouth-to-mouth resuscitation.*

I was just about to do that when his breathing picked up. Stronger. Steadier. Enough that I could feel his belly moving in and out.

Whew!

I can't tell you how relieved I was to feel that. I reached up to confirm it. And yes, I could now feel warm breath.

I have never in all my years as a doctor been so excited to feel a burst of hot air. Breath is proof of life, and young Night was breathing.

An experience like that is unsettling in a proper operating theatre. It was harrowing on the sands of chamber 8 in Tham Luang cave.

'Okay,' I said to Rick and Craig, as Mikko and Claus looked on. 'I think we're all right now. Let's get him on the stretcher and get him out of here.'

Night's breathing stayed strong, which I was profoundly grateful for. But as Mikko and Claus went off to get the stretcher, another issue developed. The boy, I could tell, was clearly starting to rouse. He was breathing harder and writhing. He was struggling with his arms behind his back, pulling at the binding around his wrists.

This I knew how to deal with. I reached into my kit, removed a syringe and gave him a booster shot in the thigh.

Keeping the balance right was key, I knew. I didn't want to under-anaesthetise him or he'd surely wake up again in the next chamber or the one after that. I didn't want to over-anaesthetise him and put him out for too long. I definitely did not want another episode like the one we'd just had. All my dose levels so far were guesswork, and this one would be guesswork, too. There was just so much we didn't know.

I still didn't know about the condition of Note, Tern and Nick – or Night, for that matter. The most perilous part of the entire cave was the passage from chamber 4 to chamber 3, just past where the ex-Navy SEAL had died and even the most experienced cave divers struggled. We had no idea what our boys might have confronted there.

20

DAY'S END

HARRY

Craig and I made better time than any of the four boy-and-diver teams who had left before us, even though their head-starts kept them comfortably in front. No more traffic jams today. We made it through the tricky passage out of chamber 4 and were swimming smoothly into chamber 3, the Thai Navy SEALs' operating base, which I thought of as our equipment warehouse. I was just lifting my head out of the water at the edge of the chamber 3 beach, when one of the American pararescue guys leaned down, slapped my helmet and said:

'Four out of four, doc.'

At first, there was so much emotion swirling inside me, I jumped straight to the worst possible interpretation – I assumed he meant four out of four had died.

These pararescuers were just awesome. They always appeared to be completely in charge, as if they could handle anything.

'It's all good,' he emphasised. 'They're all in the hospital. Everyone is okay.'

What a relief that was! I was surprised and elated and relieved, but at the same time it all seemed unreal.

The British divers were waiting for us, having handed off their boys to the bucket-brigade of Americans, Chinese and Thai medics who delivered them to the field hospital outside the entrance to the cave. So were the Euro divers. The Thai SEALs too. No one seemed in a hurry to go anywhere. We chatted with the Brits and the Euro divers, recalling some of the day's high and low points.

No one had any detailed updates on the boys yet, but the kids were said to be waking up and even talking. I couldn't imagine that Night was bright-eyed yet, but no one was hearing anything alarming or negative.

Craig and I made our way out of the cave and went directly to the Australian Federal Police compound to relax a little and catch our breath. We'd been in the cave since ten in the morning, and it was now well past eight. But even after another hour, no one seemed to know any more about the condition of the boys. Was there something we should know?

Early lessons

We trudged up to the British bunker to check in on Rick and the lads. They'd had a long day too. If I knew Rick, he'd already be thinking about how we could improve tomorrow.

It turned out there was a whole lot more to discuss than I had realised. Yes, we'd got the first four out. Yes, they seemed to be doing okay. But as we started to talk, it quickly became apparent that we still had plenty of room for improvement as we rescued the next nine Wild Boars.

Craig jumped right in. 'What was the problem with the air in the tanks?' he asked. 'It affected Harry, Rick, Jason and me, probably others too. Nobody felt right. We need clean air tomorrow.'

It sounded like a reasonable request. Far better not to poison the divers!

Claus was the one who sorted things out with the Thai sailors in charge of the compressor. Apparently, the sailors had run out of filters and so had stopped changing them. It was likely we had all received a dose of hydrocarbons, which gave us those flu-like symptoms. He and one of his diving mates helped the sailors set up a replacement compressor. 'Hopefully, it will last until we're done here.'

Some of the issues were relatively small. Someone had noticed that when the first four boys came out of the cave, the tops of their toes were scraped and bloody. Unlike the divers, who wore wetsuit booties, the boys had nothing on their feet. We all agreed to put an empty water bottle between their feet in order to float their feet off the bottom of the cave. This wasn't a life-or-death issue, but no one likes bloody toes. We just hadn't thought about it.

A bigger deal was the boys' names, and this was my fault. We could have given them hospital wristbands, or written their names on their arms with a waterproof pen. That way, when they arrived unconscious at the field hospital, the doctors and nurses would have known who they were. Apparently, it wasn't until the boys got to

Chiangrai Prachanukroh Hospital that they were identified from photos.

The Thai medical personnel team had diligently assembled the boys' medical records, including such essential details as what drugs each was allergic to, which would have given the trauma team a quick head start on whatever emergency treatments were required. Instead, they had to waste valuable minutes finding people – not the boys' family members – and asking, 'You *sure* this is Note?'

'We'll find some hospital bands for tomorrow,' I promised.

The Thai government preferred not to formally release the names of the boys who'd left the cave until all of them were out.

As soon as the first boys arrived unconscious at the field hospital, the critical-care team did what they were trained to. They tried to cut the wetsuits off.

'Hold on a second,' someone said. 'We need those wetsuits. You can't slice them to pieces.' Another detail none of us had thought of and another lesson learned.

Everyone agreed we could use more divers. 'They're coming,' Rick said.

Then there was the overall flow.

'So if we do four again tomorrow,' Rick said, 'that will leave five for the third day. Unless we added a fourth day, which I don't think anyone is in favour of. Maybe the coach would like to wait and come out with the Navy SEALs after all the boys are done. Then we could do four, four and four. He's an adult. You think he could dive out with the SEALs – dive out normally, I mean?'

I wasn't sure about that.

'I can ask,' I said. 'I'll have Pak discuss it with him.'

Then Rick and I were called into a meeting. The Thai medical people wanted to speak with us. With me, especially.

The fourth boy

In another squat building with a long folding table, half a dozen sombre-looking men sat on plastic chairs. I got the distinct impression that I wasn't being summoned to receive an award.

'What happened?' the man at the head of the table asked me in English. 'With the fourth boy.'

Night, the fourth boy, was still deeply anaesthetised, the man said. It wasn't clear when the boy would be fully awake. 'You must change the doses,' I was told in no uncertain terms.

I wasn't at all sure that lightening the ketamine dose was a good idea. We'd had four successes out of four attempts, hadn't we? Truthfully, I was expecting *high-fives* from the Thai officials – or at least some gentle *good onyas* – not a stern interrogation. Night would wake up eventually.

So I said no. 'We'll stick with what we're doing.'

Ultimately, the Thai government and the Thai medical officials had all the power, but they let me have my way.

By the end of the briefing, it was after eleven and I was completely exhausted.

Debrief

When we got back to the hotel, I said goodnight to Craig and called Fiona while I got ready for bed. She'd been glued to the telly back in Adelaide as various relatives, friends and neighbours kept popping in. She seemed deeply relieved to hear that everything had gone pretty well.

'But it could all be a weird fluke,' I said. 'We could easily kill the next four boys. I have this fear that people will start dying on day two.'

Fiona exuded her usual calm and confidence. Perhaps she thought I was being melodramatic. After the phone call, I fell asleep immediately. And somehow by Monday morning I had punched my way through most of the doubt.

21
GETTING GOOD
HARRY

We were back in the water with a story to tell, and I couldn't wait to tell it.

As soon as I arrived in chamber 9 for the second day of the rescue, I told Pak I wanted to talk to the boys. He led me up the slippery slope again. They all gathered around me on the ledge, the boys, the coach, the SEALs and Pak.

'I have some good news for you,' I said as Pak translated and everyone else just stared. 'It's about your friends. They are having a wonderful time in the hospital. They are sleeping in beds with clean sheets. They are enjoying warm showers. They are eating their favourite foods.'

The boys started rustling; smiles were breaking out.

'A lot of ice cream,' I said. 'They are all eating ice cream. They are happy and smiling and talking and laughing and playing video games.'

Okay, I might have embellished a bit.

The kids were smiling and upbeat from that point on. All of them seemed ready to give our plan a try.

On Sunday, the first rescue day, it took about three hours for the divers to bring each boy out. On Monday, we would manage to reduce that to two hours. (By Tuesday, we'd trim it even further, to ninety minutes per boy.) The teamwork got smoother. The journey and the process were that much more familiar to everyone.

Even the Thai officials were starting to relax. For the first time, Governor Narongsak Osottanakorn skipped holding a morning planning meeting. But I still felt like I was one injection away from killing a fourteen-year-old.

Talented new divers

Thankfully, Jim Warny, a 35-year-old Belgian diver (and Lufthansa electrician) now living in County Clare, Ireland, had arrived in Thailand the day before in response to Rick's call, along with Connor Roe. Connor, twenty-six, is a lance corporal in the British Army, originally from Somerset, with a permanent smile plastered across his face. The last to arrive was Josh Bratchley, twenty-seven and a meteorologist with the Met Office forecasting service. He's based on the Isle of Anglesey off the north coast of Wales. These were talented younger divers, the United Kingdom's and Ireland's next generation of cave-diving stars, happy to jump on a plane at a moment's notice – and genuinely helpful once they arrived.

By midday Monday, the three fresh arrivals were stationed at strategic points inside the cave to keep things moving and help with the top-ups as needed. Jim was in chamber 6. Josh and Connor were in chamber 5. Despite the personnel changes, our one-diver-one-boy system and our deep-sedation strategy didn't change at all. Why would we when it had worked so well?

Once back in the cave, I was growing more confident with every injection of ketamine. I was better able to judge how much each one could handle.

As Monday got busy, the three Thai Navy SEALs in chamber 9 were taking on a larger role. They had watched the British divers carefully. Now, they could prepare the kids almost as well as the Brits did. They didn't miss a trick.

The SEALs

Every day, I was more impressed by these SEALs. They didn't say much, but they were amazingly dedicated and courageous men – and not just because they had signed on for this duty without the slightest idea how long it might last or how it might end. They didn't seek personal glory. As 'operators', they couldn't even share their names. But they looked after the Wild Boars (and the rest of us) with extraordinary care and compassion, twenty-four hours a day. They were cheerful, uncomplaining, competent and hugely fit. No task, no matter how challenging or menial, was above or beneath them. More food. Another space blanket. An extra bottle of water for the night. If the SEALs had it, they would give it to the lads. They played games with the boys, creating a checkers board with rocks and dirt. None of the kids could beat the quick-thinking SEALs. And they did all this in an environment that was entirely foreign to them. Tham Luang might as well have been on the far side of the moon.

The SEALs were strong divers. From their base in the south-eastern province of Chonburi, they had trained in the open waters of the Bay of Bangkok at the northern end of the Gulf of Thailand. But cave diving was new to them.

More than 125 current and former Thai SEALs had joined the mission, many of them manning the operating base in chamber 3. Only the Thai Navy SEALs had suffered a fatality with the death of their former first-class petty officer Saman Gunan.

We'd decided not to tell the boys about Saman's death. Why upset them? But many of the SEALs did know Saman personally, and his family. Though Petty Officer Gunan hadn't done much diving in the twelve years since he'd retired, and had little if any experience in caves, he and his brothers all had the hearts of heroes. He retained all his fitness and his gung-ho spirit – and responded immediately to the call for volunteers. He was undeniably a brave and selfless man.

Perhaps the SEALs should have spent a little more time thinking about their own safety and wellbeing. It was Jason who first brought up the issue of their gas. 'You guys have enough gas to get yourselves out of here after we're finished?' he asked.

No experienced cave diver would ever swim into a cave without being certain he had sufficient air in his tanks to swim back out. But Jason's question was met with a moment of silence. 'Actually, no, we don't,' Pak said. And they were short at least one face mask.

Though they'd rushed into the cave to be helpful, it seemed they had never really considered getting out.

'When were you going to tell us this?' Rick asked under his breath. If we hadn't checked, would they have brought it up at all?

Rick told Pak not to worry. When the divers returned the next morning, we would bring in fresh air tanks for the SEALs and plant some extras on the route out, just in case. 'We're not leaving you in here,' Rick promised.

Coach Ekk

And what about Coach Ekk?

I put it to Pak. 'Instead of sedating the coach and diving him out with the boys, why don't you and the SEALs swim out with him the normal way at the end?' I asked. I was still hoping to anaesthetise as few of these guys as possible. 'He's a grown-up. I'm not sure we really need to sedate him.'

It would cut our third-day rescue count from five to four. The British divers weren't complaining, but I wasn't keen to add an extra trip.

'He'll be fine,' I assured Pak. 'See what he thinks.'

When Pak got back to me, the answer was unequivocal.

'Absolutely not,' Pak quoted Coach Ekk as telling him. 'He's been watching you take these kids out asleep. He likes the way it's going. He said thank you, but he wants to go out exactly the same way.'

Mick

Jason made the first trip out that day. He had Mick, real name Panumas Saengdee. At thirteen, he was one of the younger boys on the soccer team, though you wouldn't know it by watching him play. Mick was bigger than other kids his age and fast, with the ball-handling skills of an athletic fifteen-year-old. Because of Mick's strength in the air and his agile head skills, the coaches considered playing him as a striker, though he ended up as a defender. A student at Mae Sai Prasitsart, Mick never told his mum and dad he was going to Tham Luang. He thought they'd never give him permission. He might have some explaining to do when he got out of the cave and home to his family.

I loved learning the back stories of these boys. In so much of the media coverage, they were just 'the players', 'the boys' or 'the Wild Boars'. Like any group of young people, they had strong and distinct personalities – and bundles of charm. I was slowly getting to know them. It was hard to look at them and not think of my own wonderful children. But again there were questions when Jason and Mick reached the field hospital. 'Which one is he?' I had failed to label him. I wouldn't get this right until the third day.

Adul

John Volanthen was up next. He took fourteen-year-old midfielder and left defender Adul Samon, recognised by his fellow players as the team brainiac. He speaks five languages, plays three musical instruments and earns top marks as an eighth-grader at Ban Wiang Phan School. His language ability (Thai, Mandarin, Burmese, English and Wa) had been a huge plus when Rick and John first came upon the boys in the cave. As the only reasonable English speaker, it was Adul who was able to communicate for the stranded boys. He was distinct in at least two other ways. He was the only Christian on a team of young Buddhists, and his family was stateless, a challenging status he shared with Coach Ekk. Adul's family came from a poor hill tribe in Myanmar's self-governing Wa region. He was taken in by the Mae Sai Grace Church when he was seven years old. Soccer wasn't his only sport. For two years in a row, his volleyball team had finished second in all of northern Thailand.

Biw

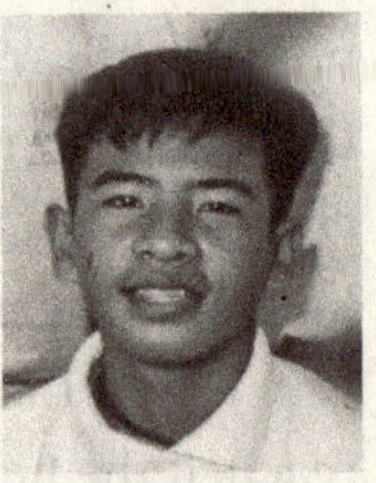

Next up was Biw, guided by Chris Jewell. Real name Ekkarat Wongsookchan, Biw is 'the Smiler'. The fourteen-year-old goalkeeper, a student at Darunratwitthaya School, had the sunniest disposition on the team. He was cheerful in victory. He was cheerful in defeat. He was even cheerful at the end of a gruelling practice, happily collecting all the soccer equipment. Once trapped in the cave, no one was surprised that Biw took it as his own personal mission to lift the spirits of the others.

Somehow, I had not only lost my glasses in the cave, but I had sat on Rick's that morning and broken them. We needed to read the syringes before I gave the drugs. I noticed Rick was rolling his index finger into a tight circle and peeking through the pinhole opening in the middle, just as I was.

'Look at us,' Rick laughed.

'Pathetic,' I agreed. 'Blind as bats.'

But you know what? We were getting it done.

Dom

Rick's boy this time was Duangphet Promthep, nickname Dom. Thirteen years old when he went into the cave, he'd turned fourteen on 3 July. Dom wasn't only a powerful striker and the highest goal-scorer on the team, he was a pint-sized version of his idol, Manchester United striker Marcus Rashford. He was also team captain, an impressive achievement for someone his age. Another Mae Sai Prasitsart student, Dom was a natural motivator, respected by his teammates. He was without a doubt one of the more talented players on the team, even invited to the junior trials for two of the leading provincial teams, Sukhothai FC and Chiangrai United FC.

As I said my goodbyes to Pak and the SEALs for the night, I had no idea how today's four boys had fared once they'd left us.

'See you tomorrow, Dr Harry,' Pak said to me as I prepared to slide into the water to swim out for the night, leaving him behind in the cave with three SEALs, four boys and a 25-year-old assistant coach. It had to be disconcerting, perhaps downright terrifying, to watch the divers all leave for the night as he and the others remained behind.

What would happen if the rains blew in?

'See you tomorrow, mate,' I answered.

Escape from the cave

Once out of the cave, we had a quick debrief with the British divers. The extra hands had made a big difference and the second day had been smoother than the first, and faster.

The early report on the second-day's boys was entirely positive. A couple of them were already on their way to the big hospital in Chiang Rai, we were told. After the debrief, Craig and I plopped ourselves down in the Australian tent for a few minutes of relaxation with the AFP guys before we'd head back to the hotel to collapse. For dinner, we had pizza and a sports drink.

Then, someone said excitedly, 'The prime minister is coming. You have to stay around to meet him.'

Really?

One of the AFP guys leaned over to me and whispered, 'Prayut Chan-o-cha,' which I took to be the prime minister's name. 'He's a retired general.' Apparently, he'd been PM since 2014. 'He's taken quite an interest in the rescue,' I was told. 'You all have to line up, and he will shake your hands.'

I found Michael Costa, our trusty DFAT handler. 'We've got to get out of here,' I told him. 'If I don't get some sleep, I'm not going to be able to function tomorrow.'

Craig was even more direct. 'We need to get home and get to bed. In future, Harry can brief somebody, and they can give our report at whatever meetings they have. They can meet the prime minister. This isn't safe for anybody, keeping us up all night then going into the cave for another ten hours the next day.'

Michael sounded sympathetic, but there was a hitch. 'The road's been closed by security because the prime minister is coming up.'

That's when I had a true moment of genius.

'All right,' I said to Michael. 'We all get into one of those ambulances. We put the flashing lights on, and we go down the hill. Can you organise it?'

'Okay,' he said. 'Let's try.'

Michael went off and found one of the Thai medical people and explained that we needed an ambulance so we could get home to bed.

The answer came back straightaway: *Whatever Dr Harry needs.*

Michael snuck us through the dark to where the ambulances were parked. We had a clear view of the road out, which was all lit up for the prime minister's arrival with soldiers lined up on either side.

'Craig,' I said, 'you jump in the back and I'll jump in the front.'

I'd tried to outsmart Craig but I think he got the better spot. He opened the sliding door on the side of the ambulance, and ten Thai nurses, each more beautiful than the others, were sitting there. I took out my phone and began taking pictures of Craig and the nurses. Soon, they were giggling, hugging Craig, posing for photos and bringing out their own phones.

'*Woo hoo!*' Craig called out as the ambulance pulled onto the main road. We flew past the security barriers and the lines of soldiers back to our border-side hotel.

I know Heather appreciated it when I texted some of the nurse photos to her in Perth.

22

OLD BOY

HARRY

'Miracle in the Cave' headlines were blasting around the world – as if any of this were a miracle and not the result of plain old human effort and ingenuity. Governor Narongsak Osottanakorn, the rescue coordinator, told a packed press conference: 'For the next rescue we believe it will be a 100 per cent success.'

Craig and I were both eager to fuel up on Tuesday morning for the big day ahead. We kept getting better at this, but we also faced fresh challenges – we'd be trying to dive out with four boys *and* the coach, and everyone was expecting us to succeed.

Rising water

The walk into the cave that morning was more sombre than usual. It had rained a lot overnight. There was talk of more rain to come. Rick and John had been there early enough to see the cave in full flood, swirling brown rapids that drove even the fittest and most skilled divers back, threatening to pin them into a crevice or under a ledge. No one wanted to die that way.

At an opportune rest break in the dry-cave section, we stopped to quickly talk it through. 'Is this safe or not?' I asked. 'You guys have the experience in this cave. What do you want to do?'

It was Rick who spoke up. 'Let's look at the water-level device in the next chamber,' he said. 'If it's risen, that could mark the start of significant flooding. If it's okay, we proceed. If there is any sense that water is rising at any stage inside the cave, we bail and come straight out. Even one centimetre change. Agreed?'

Craig wasn't so sure. He took the view that if the water levels did rise, we would still be able to get out with the flow, even if we couldn't get through to chamber 9. But we ultimately accepted Rick's cautious recommendation. We caught up with Chris and Jason. They agreed.

Luckily the water rose no more.

That morning, several of the divers, including Craig and I, had decided to take extra cylinders with us. That way, the SEALs would have plenty of gas for even a slow dive out. Given their inexperience with cave diving, we didn't expect any speed records. On the way in, they'd taken twice as long to reach the boys as Rick and John had, breathing their way through most of their four cylinders. Now they'd be able to breathe their way out.

Chamber 9

'I would recommend you dive out one at a time, not all

bunched together,' I said to Pak once we made it back to chamber 9. He shared this advice with the others. 'Leave plenty of space between each man. Also, wait a couple of hours after I leave, so the water clears up for you.' If there was a hold-up with any of the boys on the way out, I didn't want extra divers piling up behind them to complicate the situation. Frankly, I also didn't want the SEALs anywhere near me when I was making my own exit at the end of the day.

They listened carefully to my explanation with their usual polite respect. They spoke earnestly among themselves. Then, Pak delivered the verdict. 'We are a team. We will come out together as a team. That is what they say.'

Since we had five Wild Boars to rescue today, we had to adjust the diver line-up. Jason would take the first one, but only as far as chamber 8. From there, Jim Warny would ferry that one out the rest of the way. Jason would then swim back to chamber 9 and handle the fifth (and final) trip of the day. John, Rick and Chris would ferry the second, third and fourth.

We also needed to label the boys with their names. I'd brought a waterproof marker along for the SEALs to write each boy's name on his arm.

And there was an issue with the face masks. We had only four masks that we knew were a good size and effective for the boys. We would take the next two best masks with us to give us some options.

First boy of the day

When the day's first young traveller came down the slope, he was suited up like all the rest of them in a small-size wetsuit, buoyancy collar and hood. He had the bungees around his midsection and the cable ties on his wrists. John helped me prepare him for the trip.

'Hello, little fella,' I said as the youngster settled onto my knee and I continued with the preparations for his long journey ahead. 'How are you feeling today?'

'Okay,' he said softly.

'I'm gonna jab you a couple of times – good boy, good boy.'

He wasn't too chatty, but Pak was there to translate when I needed him. With my usual banter, I tried to distract my young patient from the two needles he was about to receive. I cuddled him and tried to be soothing. It wouldn't be much longer, I knew, until he slipped into sweet unconsciousness.

'How old are you?' I asked.

'Twenty-five,' he answered.

I thought he was messing with me.

'Oh, yeah,' I said with a smile. 'I'm twenty-five too.'

'And what position do you play on the soccer team?'

'Coach.' Pak was translating for both of us.

'I am a famous soccer coach back in Australia,' I said, playing along with the obvious ruse.

'No, really, Dr Harry,' Pak interrupted. 'He's the coach. Coach Ekk.'

'*What?!*' I sputtered, laughing at my screw-up. John, who was holding the face mask, smiled and shook his head at me. 'You idiot, Harry.' In the background, the ever-efficient Jason was getting geared up for the trip.

It was only then that I looked closely under the boy's

diving hood. He wasn't a boy at all. I could see a few wispy hairs growing out of his 25-year-old chin.

In my defence, the coach was definitely smaller than a couple of his players.

Maybe he was afraid we would leave him to swim out with the SEALs and he wasn't taking any chances.

'Ready for a jab, mate?' I asked in my best, deep, blokey voice to the grown man who was still sitting on my knee.

Tee

After Jason headed into the water with the youthful coach, it was John's turn. I waited a decent interval – no more traffic jams, please – before asking Pak to send the next one down the hill. He turned out to be the big boy, sixteen-year-old defender Phonchai Khamluang, nickname Tee. A studious pupil at the Ban Pa Yang School, Tee was the largest of the Wild Boars. Quiet, tidy, eager to work hard, he is a member of the school council and a volunteer traffic director each morning. Like Coach Ekk and two of the other boys, he is stateless. Tee and his family are Tai Yai, members of a marginalised tribe originally from Shan state in neighbouring Myanmar. That has made life difficult for the family any time they have tried to find work, own property or travel.

Jab, jab, dress and go: by now, this little system of ours was running like a well-oiled machine. I had finally begun to believe we just might achieve the impossible. Over the past two days, the chatter up on the ledge had grown quieter. We'd started with thirteen Wild Boars, and now only three boys remained. Suddenly, I heard a burst of laughter mixed with raised voices.

Pak always seemed to have a smile on his face, but now he was almost chuckling. The SEALs, he explained, had caught the boys stuffing American MREs into their wetsuits.

'They like the flavours,' he said. 'Very much. They have a new favourite food.'

Titan

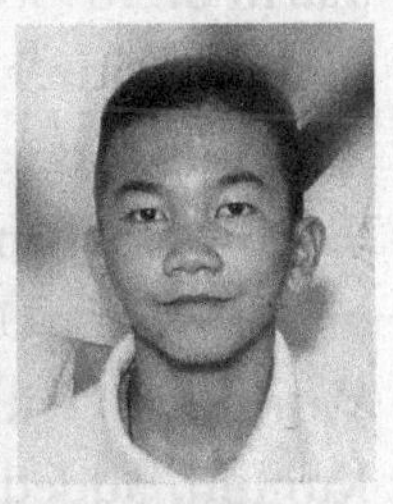

Rick would dive out with the boy known as Titan, Chanin Wiboonrungrueang, at eleven the youngest Wild Boar. A forward on the soccer team, Titan was in his final year at Anubanmaesai primary school and lives near Thailand's border with Myanmar. When he was ten, he spent time as a schoolboy monk, and photos of him with shaven head and saffron robes still hung in the family home. Though his grandmother, Yod Kantawong, is stateless and his hairdresser mother was born in Myanmar, his mum married a Thai salesman and became eligible for Thai citizenship. So Titan was born a Thai citizen, free to ride his bicycle across the border to visit relatives on both sides. Sadly, his grandmother enjoyed no such privilege. When her grandson went missing, she had to apply for a special visitor's slip to rush across the border. Titan and his family were very close to Coach Ekk. When his parents were away, Titan often stayed with Ekk and his aunt.

The first three dives of the day – Coach Ekk's, Tee's and Titan's – all went like clockwork. Practice really was making perfect. As it turned out, we weren't even close to finished.

Pong

Chris Jewell would dive out with thirteen-year-old Somphong Jaiwong, Pong to his friends. A right-winger and midfielder on the team and a student at Mae Sai Prasitsart, Pong was one of those boys who always made sure his friends were comfortable, happy and having a good time. He had an alarm on his watch, letting the others know if it was day or night outside.

Pong was raised by his Uncle Chai after his father died. 'He's football mad and spends all his spare time playing or watching,' Uncle Chai marvelled. 'He was watching the World Cup with me before this.' His teacher, Manutsanun Kuntun, added: 'He dreams of becoming a footballer for the Thai national team.' And he had shown some talent too. Outside the cave, Uncle Chai posed proudly with the string of medals the boy had won playing soccer with his pals.

Such moving, human stories. Now, Pong was finally on his way home.

Mark

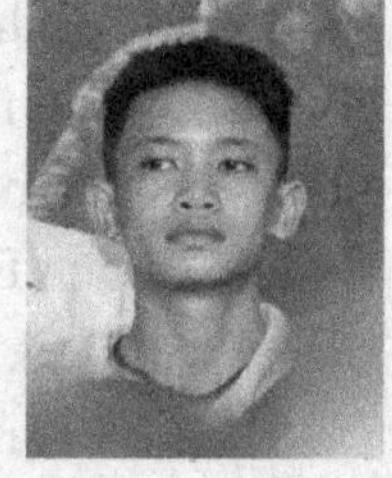

For three straight days, Mark, real name Mongkol Boonpiam, thought he was about to leave. He'd bravely volunteered to be one of the first to put on the diving gear and make the long journey out. Now he would be the last boy out of the cave.

Mark was another stateless boy, though he did have some hope of eventually earning Thai citizenship. Mark's parents were born in Myanmar, but they had lived in Thailand for ten years already, and he was born there. A bright, athletic seventh-grader at Ban Pa Muat School, he studied with almost the same enthusiasm he brought to swimming, cycling, volleyball and, especially, soccer. He'd been playing soccer since he was in kindergarten and loved the sport so much he was rarely seen without a football shirt. He was on the same volleyball team as his Wild Boar teammate Adul.

At thirteen years old, Mark was listed on the team roster as trainee. He wasn't the youngest boy on the team, but he was easily the tiniest, and that created one last complication for him. We didn't have a decent mask small enough. What we did have was a tiny pink child's mask, little more than a toy. But that seemed too impossibly fragile to be safe. It also lacked the all-important positive-pressure function that we had come to rely on. The other option was a full-sized, grey, AGA commercial-diver's mask designed for a large man.

I was shocked to see such a diminutive figure, dressed in dive gear, come wobbling down the slope. Why was he so tiny? I thought we had sent out the smallest of the kids already. And here I was now, faced with what appeared to be the smallest of them all!

'Who's this?' I asked Pak in horror. 'What's his weight?'

'Mark is his name,' Pak told me. 'He was thirty kilos when he came in.'

The boy standing in front of me looked far smaller than thirty kilograms. He was the smallest by far. And we had only the two untested masks to use. We had no choice. For all I knew, the rain was now bucketing down outside, and all our lives were in significant danger. Mark had to leave the cave, today.

I cracked on and injected his leg with ketamine, adjusting the dose for his delicate stature. Minutes later, he was asleep, and Jason stepped forwards, initially proffering the positive-pressure AGA. There was just no way. It was gaping all around Mark's little face. It would never keep the water out or the air in. We tried the little pink mask. Time was ticking by, and we had to get the mask to seal. With no positive pressure, any trickle of water into the mask could easily drown the boy. The soft, silicone skirt seemed horribly delicate. The whole mask was just flopping around. After ten minutes of refitting, padding out Mark's face with foam and getting the best seal possible, Jason looked into my eyes. We realised we could do no more. If we mucked around further, Mark would get dangerously hypothermic and would need another top up of ketamine. It was now or never. So close to total success, we were looking at certain disaster.

It was up to Jason now. All he could do was dive Mark out. Once he started, he would have to keep moving, finally appearing at chamber 3 with a tiny corpse or a living boy. My heart sank for the hundredth time as the pair swam down the canal towards home.

23
LAST OUT
HARRY

I began what I knew would be my final dive out, moving with the current, kicking as I went, hand over hand, methodically down the line. My fourth day in the water, I was finally feeling like I had some mastery over Tham Luang. Craig was up ahead of me. Mikko and Claus were with him. Chris and Jason were up there somewhere with their boys. Jim and the Coach, Rick's kid and John's kid, I told myself, should already be at the field hospital by now. Everyone was heading in the same direction.

Out. All the way out.

Only Pak and the SEALs remained behind in chamber 9.

I stopped briefly to say hello to a couple of the guys still waiting at their assigned stations. Erik was just sitting in the mud with his thoughts. He seemed like a great guy. Calm. Solid. Unshaken by the previous days' events.

On I swam, wanting to distance myself from the combat swimmers who'd be following.

Lost

As I moved through the relative ease of chamber 4, I steeled myself for what I knew was still waiting for me, the final, tough section of the cave, the tightly constricted passage connecting chambers 4 and 3. But even before I got there, I heard a voice in the darkness ahead of me.

'Harry? Harry? Is that you?'

It was Chris. He sounded distressed.

'Yeah,' I called back. 'Are you all right? Is the kid okay?'

'The kid's fine,' Chris answered. 'It's me. Come down if you can.' As quickly as I was able to kick and pull, I raced down the line towards Chris. There he was in the water with the kid floating next to him, face down, bubbling away happily. But Chris looked white as a sheet.

'I dropped the line,' he said. 'I've been lost for fifteen minutes. I got all turned around.'

Chris is usually super cool and highly experienced. But as he explained it to me, he'd just had the nearest near-miss a cave diver can have. And it happened at the nastiest, narrowest part of the cave.

Before he and Pong got this far, Chris said, Jason and his boy, Mark, had caught up to them. Jason, I believe, helped Chris top up Pong, who appeared to be rousing and needed another dose. Jason and Mark then moved ahead of them, flipping the order of the last two teams out. Now, Chris and Pong would be the final pair leaving the cave.

In this section, the line is on your left side. At one point there is a classic line trap, where the line goes into a section that is too small for a human to follow. You have to extend your arm out to hold the line as it gets pulled around a left-hand corner. At that point, the cave is really narrow before it opens up again, and you need to fit your body through a small vertical slot. Feeling far to the right, you find the slot and try to get through it without letting go of the line on your left. It is almost an unsolvable puzzle on your own. Add an anaesthetised child to the equation, and it is amazing there hadn't already been an accident here. You're doing it all blind. You're pulling the line as you swim through the cave, but it's very easy to drop it.

Apparently, that's exactly what happened to Chris.

He had been searching desperately for the line and couldn't find it. All he'd found so far was an electrical cable on the floor of the cave. *This has to go somewhere,* he reasoned. *I'll just follow it out.* Unfortunately, he followed the cable in the opposite direction, deeper *into* the cave. When he finally surfaced, he wasn't sure where he was. In chamber 4? In some side alcove? He couldn't even tell any more which way was in and which was out. He couldn't find the guide line. He was truly lost.

Fifteen minutes in the dark with a limited supply of air and a sedated child who needs to get out of the cave can feel like a lifetime, and not a very pleasant one. Chris was stranded in chamber 4, trying to gather himself, when he saw my light coming through.

'Okay,' I told him, 'no worries. You sit here. Take all the time you need. I will hand you the line. Let yourself calm down. Come out when you're ready. I'll take the kid through.'

Chris immediately passed the boy to me.

I was secretly pleased to be able to escort one of the anaesthetised kids through part of the cave. Over three draining days, I had been sedating them, prepping them for their risky journeys and passing them off to Rick, John, Jason and Chris. Now, after all that, I would finally get to dive one of the kids out myself. Now, I thought to myself, it will feel like I've done a bit of everything.

How little I knew about *everything*.

The line

I pulled the kid close to me and got a firm hold of the line. Together, we started moving along the same path that Chris had. We got to the exact spot where Chris came unstuck, the super-tight passage where chamber 4 leads into chamber 3. It's a dicey part of the cave, so I approached with extra care.

I grabbed the line and placed it under the crook of my arm, holding it securely in my armpit. What could be safer than that? Then, I changed sides with the boy, so we could both get through this narrow hole.

I was ready to dive us through when I thought: *Okay, where's the line?*

Where is it? I just had it. No! I can't find the line! I took a breath to steady myself. I still couldn't find the line. *You idiot! Exactly the same thing has now happened to me!*

I did what twenty-five years of cave diving had taught me, and didn't lose my cool. *Stop, breathe, think, ACT.* I went into my lost-line search drill. I stayed right where I was. I tried not to move in any direction. I made sure I had a solid grip on the boy so he wouldn't float off as I hunted for the missing line.

I made large circles with my arms. Nothing. If the line was out there, I was going to find it. I forced myself to stay calm. Panic kills more divers than empty cylinders and falling rocks combined. The line had to be nearby.

I did the same thing on my left side, and then on my right. Still no line.

I was sitting in the dark. Even with a top-up dose of ketamine, the kid wouldn't stay out forever. We had to get out of there.

I reached around on the floor again. This time, I felt electrical cable, possibly the same bit that Chris had found. My mind went to the same place that his did. *Oh, well, at least I know which way is out. I can follow the cable out rather than going back in.* I was feeling stupid and frightened too.

Suddenly, I moved my arm, and there was the line.

It was in my armpit, exactly where it had been all this time.

Now my feelings of stupidity were seasoned with deep relief. For the rest of the dive, I never let go of the rope again.

I did smack my head a few more times on the limestone. It was hard to avoid. The stalactites hung low and unpredictably in that part of the cave, and I was trying to protect the boy. Through the very narrowest stretch, I nestled him right under my chin, protecting him but turning my head into a battering ram. Even with my helmet on, the blows were jarring.

Then we were scooting along the line with the current as we approached chamber 3. We had the water flow behind us. I was just following the line.

I was kicking with my fins, reaching out blindly in front of me as we went. When I held my breath, I could hear Pong breathing steadily, the bubbles coming up past my face. It was a fabulous sound, proof of all we had struggled to achieve. With an arm around his belly I could feel every breath. It felt right.

The whirring of the electric pumps told me how close we were to chamber 3. It was a welcome sound, but it also made me slightly nervous. I thought: *I really don't want to put my fingers into those pump blades.* Most pumps have screens over the suction part to protect careless divers, but we were sharing cave water with the fierce suction power of massive pumps.

Then suddenly, my head popped out of the water, and bright light hit my eyes. That's when I knew Pong and I were just about home.

In that flash, people were all over us. Yelling. Cheering. Laughing. Clapping. Shouting 'All right!' and 'Way to go!' and 'You made it!' and all kinds of other stuff I couldn't comprehend.

The first hands I felt were those of three big, strong, American pararescuers, who jumped into the water with us. 'Hey, doc,' I heard one of them say. 'Well done, man!'

They were all patting me on the back. One of them grabbed the kid. In an instant, the boy was gone, onto a stretcher, through chamber 3, out of the cave and up the hill to the field hospital, where a team of Thai doctors and nurses was waiting for him. He hadn't stirred at all.

They're all out

'Is everyone all right?' I asked.

'You bet,' one of the Americans answered. 'They're all out. They're all fine.'

For a moment, things turned quiet in my head. In that brief moment of silence, it was almost like I was staring down at myself in the water, trying to make sense of it all.

Wow, I thought. *It's over.* Unless something went wrong with one of the kids in the next half hour, everyone was going to be well. All I could do was climb out of the water and share the glorious feeling with those who had helped to make it happen.

Rick and the other British divers stepped forwards. Then there was Craig, flashing the biggest smile. Without him, I knew, we never could have rescued these boys. We were a team, then and now. Chris was still behind me, but I was sure he'd arrive shortly. Erik and some of the others began to appear. And soon, it seemed like almost everyone was there. The American pararescuers. The Chinese. The Thai military people and volunteers, the ones who had been managing chamber 3. They were standing around with giant smiles on their faces.

I have never won the lottery before, but I'll bet it doesn't feel any more exhilarating than this. I was nervous. I was numb. And I realised my life would never be the same.

Someone passed around a drink bottle and somebody else found some paper cups.

'To us,' the great Rick Stanton said as the little paper cups were raised in the air. 'And to the boys.' I swear even Jason Mallinson cracked a smile.

Someone passed around a bucket of fried chicken. No one seemed eager to leave.

Then Claus spoke up.

'You know,' he said, 'the SEALs are still in there, Dr Pak and his guys.'

That was true. At least now they had the air to swim out. Before they left chamber 9, Pak and the SEALs wanted to let the silt settle, and to avoid any human traffic jams. It would have been easier if they had left singly or in pairs, but they were a team. They wanted to travel together.

Finally, a few minutes before 11 p.m., everyone was out of the cave.

V
LIVING

24
CALL HOME
HARRY

I texted Fiona as soon as Craig and I left the cave.

'All out,' I wrote. 'Might be celebrating. Call you when back at the hotel.'

On each of the past three nights I had texted Fiona as soon as I was safely outside. Craig checked in with Heather as well. He and I were always exhausted, desperate for sleep. But there were always things to do first, so it was late by the time Fiona and I could speak.

I had come to treasure those bleary phone chats. When your emotions are running wild, talking to a calm, loving spouse saves your sanity.

Craig and I just wanted to have a quiet celebration with our mates. With the pressure and the craziness of the past few days, this might be our only opportunity to hang out and bond.

The rain had set in consistently now. But it didn't matter. Everyone was out of the cave. Just a few hours earlier, rain could have been a catastrophe. Now, who cared?

Heading to the van, we couldn't escape the congratulations. My hands were sore from being vigorously shaken by so many well-wishers.

I've got something to tell you

Meanwhile, more than 7000 kilometres away in Adelaide, a drama had been unfolding that I knew nothing about.

On Sunday night, after the first four boys were out of the cave, my eldest sister, Amanda, called to tell Fiona that Dad was in hospital. He rallied, and was up and dressed and back in his nursing-home room next day, seeming totally fine.

On Tuesday night, Fiona texted Amanda to share the great news: 'Harry's out. Everyone's fine. We can all relax now.'

Amanda texted back: 'I'm just going to pop round for a hug.' It was nearly eleven when Amanda and her husband, Richard, arrived.

'Fi,' she said. 'I've got something else to tell you.'

Fiona knew straightaway what it was going to be.

'Dad died,' Amanda said.

Fiona had to prepare herself for one of the toughest conversations she'd ever have to have.

She went in and told our younger son Charlie that his papa had died and gave him a hug. Our older son James had already gone to sleep, preparing for an early start. Our daughter Millie was in Connecticut.

Her first thought was to spare me the news that night,

but then she thought: *I don't want him finding out on Facebook or TV. I have to tell him tonight.*

It was 11.30 p.m. Thai time, two in the morning in Adelaide, when I finally got back to the hotel. I was sure Fiona would still be waiting up for me.

Craig had the room next to mine, but his shower was broken, so he asked if he could come in and use mine.

'Go for it, mate,' I said, as I settled onto the edge of the bed and reached for my phone. I heard Fiona say hello.

'Everyone's out,' I said. 'Everyone.'

'I know,' she told me. 'That's wonderful. I'm so happy for you. And for the kids. The news is everywhere.'

I was excited, and exhausted. I hardly drew a breath. Fiona let me keep on talking.

Then, finally, she said: 'There's something else. It's your dad.'

It was her tone of voice as much as the words she said. I knew immediately that my father was dead.

Talk about clashing emotions.

'What happened?' I asked.

He had dinner in his room, Fiona said, then the nurse offered him a cuppa at 7.15. At 7.45 she found him on the floor, dead.

He looked perfectly peaceful.

Just then, Craig came out of the shower. I managed a quick, 'See you, mate. See you in the morning.' I didn't want him to see me cry.

He didn't linger.

I collapsed on the bed and broke down completely. Poor Fiona had to listen to me sobbing on the phone.

I knew Dad had been following the reports from Thailand on the TV news with updates when Amanda and others went to visit. The local paper featured my ugly mug on the front page one day, and no doubt he'd have bragged to the staff and residents about his son being over there.

I told Craig the next morning at breakfast, but nobody else.

When I did step outside, the triumph of the rescue had everyone smiling. It was like a load had been lifted off the entire nation, off the entire world. It felt nice to know I had played a part.

My father's death wouldn't stay secret for long, and when Glen McEwen, the Australian Federal Police manager for Asia, came up to me, I could tell he knew. He just gave me a giant bear hug, and that was it. I really cried. I needed a hug at that moment.

Prime Minister Turnbull calling

'Prime Minister Turnbull wants to have a Skype call with the Australians who were directly involved in the rescue,' Glen said. 'He especially wants to say hello to you.'

'I'm not up to it,' I said.

But Glen said it was important. Everyone would be there.

'I might lose it if he says something to me,' I told Glen. 'Tell him not to single me out.'

Glen agreed to pass the message on.

They'd set up a laptop for the Skype call in a tiny hotel room. I hid in the back of the crowd, as Malcolm Turnbull came on the screen from Canberra.

'Good morning, everyone,' he said cheerfully, then added straightaway: 'Is Dr Harris there?'

Oh, no! Suddenly, all these big coppers were shuffling me to the front and sitting me down, dead centre.

'Good morning, sir,' I said.

'I'm sorry for your loss,' the prime minister declared.

It was amazing how quickly that news spread.

Julie Bishop, the foreign-affairs minister, said something, and there it was, in the little words crawling across the bottom on the CNN screen: 'Cave rescuer's father dies in Australia. Jim Harris, Adelaide surgeon.'

But it made me smile. *Dad's on the telly!* I thought. He would have loved that.

Soon enough, I was also able to see the happy side of things. The kids were all out of the cave. My father had died the way he wanted to. I was happy for them and for him. I didn't want to go home right away. It didn't seem right. I needed to spend time with the people I'd shared this experience with and get to know them in slightly more normal circumstances. My father, if anyone, would understand.

25
HIGH FIVES
HARRY

'We'd really just like to walk around town and relax,' I said to the ever-present Michael Costa. We needed it, given how much pressure we'd all been under.

The celebrating began even before the sun went down. It started with a lavish poolside barbecue at Le Méridien Chiang Rai Resort, an elegant riverside hotel with lush gardens and beautiful grounds. The American parajumpers were there. So were the Brits and the Europeans and a bunch of other people. The hotel laid out a fantastic spread and no one could stop smiling, it seemed.

A bit of a blur

After that it all became a bit of a blur. I remember a big outdoor restaurant where a general was up on stage with a Thai country and western band, singing at the top of his voice! The restaurant had a huge buffet of spicy Thai food and although it was all a bit surreal, it was the perfect way to relax.

Then it was on to a massive nightclub, where a boy band was playing, lights were flashing and people were dancing wildly. More people kept coming over, shaking our hands and thanking us.

About one in the morning, I realised we had had enough. We managed to find our way outside. Only then did I realise: *Oh, we don't know where we're staying, or how we're getting there, or where our gear and our clothes are.*

Then things started happening as if by magic. Two men hustled us into a van, and off we went into the warm Chiang Rai night. Who were these men? Where were they taking us? We did not know. But soon after we pulled into a hotel we'd never seen before. It was plush and beautiful, much nicer than the border-side joint where we'd been staying, and somehow all our stuff was already in our rooms.

The next morning, Craig and I both felt a bit quiet at breakfast. Glen McEwen sauntered over to our table and said cheerfully: 'Morning, boys. How are you?'

'Not bad,' Craig said. 'No idea whatsoever how we got home last night though.'

The chief smiled at that. 'See those blokes over there?'

Half a dozen Thai police officers were finishing breakfast nearby. They looked far more alert than we did as they smiled and waved.

'They're the Thai tourist police. They were with you all night. They brought you home.'

And we'd thought we were out on the town having the time of our lives, and we actually had babysitters all night.

Hospital visit

The boys were all at Chiangrai Prachanukroh Hospital, where they had been taken variously by helicopter or ambulance. I was eager to see the kids, so I asked Kittanu to try to organise a visit.

'Not even the parents are being allowed to go in,' Kittanu reported back. 'The boys are in some kind of quarantine.'

Quarantine?

But by early afternoon, we heard we could drop into the hospital if we wanted to.

After arriving in the DFAT van, Craig and I were greeted by a stern-looking woman in a green military uniform: 'matron'. She was polite but clearly was not putting up with any nonsense.

There were some parents upstairs, but they weren't with their children. All they could do was gaze at their sons through a window on the far side of a locked door. After more than two emotionally gruelling weeks they couldn't even touch them.

The hospital staffers insisted we both wear surgical masks before they led us into a large open ward, where Coach Ekk and the boys were lying in hospital beds in matching, loose-fitting white-print gowns with surgical masks on their faces or dangling around their necks.

There were TVs on, and some of the boys had hand-held video-game consoles. It was lunchtime, and every boy had a tray with hand sanitiser and four or five bowls of food, which they were shovelling down with gusto.

Their smiles were brilliant. We walked from bed to bed saying 'hello'.

Everyone said 'hello' back to us in English and also greeted us with a head-bowing *wai*. To me, the *wai* is one of the sweetest things about being in Thailand. Thais execute that gesture as a friendly greeting, as an expression of affection, as a simple acknowledgement and as a sign of deep respect. Usually accompanied by a slight knee-bend and a pacific smile, the *wai* has meanings I cannot even comprehend. There are similar gestures elsewhere in South-East Asia and in parts of India, but nowhere is it such a part of life as in Thailand, where even Ronald McDonald clasps his hands in a *wai*.

We made our way around the sterile white room, stopping at each and every bed, and shaking the boys' warm little hands. A woman translated for us as we asked how they were feeling, what they'd had to eat in the hospital and what was the first thing they wanted to do when they got home.

We spent some extra time with Adul, the one boy who spoke some English. He was eager to tell us how he and his teammates had reacted when they first realised they were trapped in the cave.

The water kept rising

'The water blocked our way,' Adul said, demonstrating with a gesture. 'When we tried to leave, we couldn't go out. Then, the water kept rising, and we had to run back into the cave and find a higher place to go.'

The team members spent the first night in an area that sounded like chamber 8. 'But the water was still coming up the next morning,' Adul said. 'So we had to go more far.

That was the high place where we stayed until Dr Harry jabbed us and made us sleep and sent us out.'

I didn't conduct any medical examinations on the boys, but none of them appeared unhealthy at all, beyond the random sniffles and scratchy throats you'd find in any middle-school class.

Coach Ekk, still the leader, was all smiles and seemed extra-pleased. After a warm bow, he grinned widely and gave me a strong handshake, looking deeply into my eyes. It was Ekk, in those early days, who had cared for these children completely on his own. He saved their lives before anyone else had a chance to. It was hard to hold back the tears in my emotionally fragile state.

I expected the boys to be shy around us, but they looked us in the eye and gave big, broad smiles. They all appeared to remember who we were, even though they'd only ever seen us in full diving gear. No one seemed to object to us being there before their parents. We'd shared something extraordinary and death-defying, and all of us had come through alive.

Minutes later, I turned around and saw Pak, somehow making the same hospital gown look sharp, striding towards me. Without saying a word, we enveloped each other in a big bear-hug. It was almost overwhelming. I couldn't easily express my gratitude at having another medical man in the cave with me to share the burden of this grave undertaking. We had counted on each other so much. He was the other, true grown-up – a phenomenal bloke – always smiling, always happy, always upbeat, the consummate role model and leader. Clear, calm, focused – a natural motivator.

I could understand why his troops were so fond of him and why the boys seemed to trust him unreservedly. When you were with him, you felt that everything was going to be fine.

I felt like Pak and I would be friends for the rest of our lives. Apparently, he felt the same.

EPILOGUE

'HEALTHY, HAPPY, SMILEY'

HARRY

Craig and I hitched a ride home on a Royal Australian Air Force transport plane, which was sent to scoop up all the Aussie government people who had helped in Thailand. Sitting in the back of that massive Boeing C-17 Globemaster III was really my first chance to reflect on the extraordinary events of the past eight days. What an adventure it had turned out to be, the diving kind and the human kind. How proud we were of all we had accomplished, even with the sad news about my dad.

From what I heard later, he and everyone at the nursing home watched the rescue on television. Fiona and my sisters took the newspapers to him and pointed out the front-page stories. He seemed to grasp I was off on another of my cave-diving adventures, and that we were trying to help some stranded children in Thailand.

Farewell Dad

Nobody wanted a huge, formal funeral. Not for Jim Harris. We had the simplest ceremony possible, just for close family. I said a few words and so did my sisters. My children and their cousins stood up and spoke. They were all very close to their papa. To them, he was always the bloke who made everyone laugh.

Then, we had the real send-off. My dad would have loved every minute of it, every last laugh and raised glass. It was just a brilliant event. All his old mates were there along with the next generation and the next generation after that. Everyone was talking and laughing and having a grand old time. I wish Dad could have been there, and Mum, too. It was a truly perfect send-off for a wonderful man.

He was eighty-eight. He had as full a life as anyone could hope for. He was a wonderful father and a treasured friend. He even got to share in his son's greatest adventure. What more could anyone ask?

Home at last

All thirteen of the boys were discharged from Chiangrai Prachanukroh Hospital on Wednesday, 18 July, after a full week of quarantine, observation and many large meals. 'My own bed felt warm,' said Duangpetch Promthep, the boy known as Dom, whose first home-cooked meal was stewed pork knuckles over rice. There had been nothing like that in the cave, not even the tasty American MREs that several of the boys tried to smuggle out. Since he had turned thirteen on 3 July – one of four Wild Boars (along with Night, Nick and Note) to have a birthday in the cave – Dom finally got to blow out the candles on his cake.

But Thai officials were still worried about the boys' mental health. Eleven of the boys – all except for the Christian Adul – joined Coach Ekk in a week-long Buddhist retreat at a local temple. Their heads were shaved. They dressed in traditional robes. They prayed. They meditated. They spent time in quiet reflection. And before they returned to their families on 25 July, Coach Ekk was ordained a monk and the players novices. They dedicated their retreat to Saman Gunan, the former Thai Navy SEAL who died helping to rescue them.

Biw's mother thought all this was nice, up to a point. 'We can only do this for nine days,' she said. 'Then, he has to go back to study and prepare for exams, back to his normal life.'

Whether or not this helped the boys, it kept them away from the international media. On 6 August, the boys were welcomed to Mae Sai Prasitsart School. They received new uniforms from the school management and red Bayern Munich football jerseys from a German club. Brightly coloured threads were tied around their wrists, a traditional *bai si* ritual meant to signify moral support. Then, the boys were given make-up classes for all the schoolwork they'd missed.

Something momentous

On 8 August, something truly momentous occurred.

A small ceremony was held in Mae Sai. Adul, Mark, Tee and Coach Ekk, the four stateless Boars, stood together.

Each of them was promised fast-track citizenship and given a Thai national identification card. This process normally takes up to ten years, when it happens at all. With the new ID cards, the four could travel freely, work legally in various professions and receive access to public services such as health care.

'We are very, very happy,' Tee's father, Inn Khamluang, said afterwards. The family had already been waiting for three or four years, since Tee was in the sixth grade.

The drama faded just as slowly for us. Reporters kept calling Craig and me and showing up at our homes. School groups and business associations invited us to speak. There was talk of books and movies and other crazy stuff. People kept using the H-word, and the awards started pouring in. There was the Star of Courage, which honours 'acts of conspicuous courage in circumstances of great peril'. We were given the Medal of the Order of Australia, which is a very formal thing established in the 1970s by Queen Elizabeth II. It was a special thrill for me to receive the Edgar Pask Citation from the Association of Anaesthetists of Great Britain and Ireland, named for the medical pioneer whose bold experiments on himself in the water had inspired me.

Then Craig and I were named regional winners for Australian of the Year, Craig for Western Australia, me for South Australia. The award celebrates Australians in any fields who work to improve Australia or the planet.

In January, all thirty-two of the state winners, four from each state or territory, were invited with our families to a three-day shindig at the capital in Canberra. Well, blow me down if we didn't win. Prime Minister Scott Morrison made the announcement, keeping the suspense until the last second. We were praised for our 'selflessness, courage and willingness to help others in a time of need'. Apparently, we embodied 'the very best of the Australian spirit.'

In my acceptance speech, I raised a larger issue Craig and I had both been thinking about.

'I am proud to call myself an explorer,' I said. 'But I do fear for kids today who, living in a risk-averse society, will not learn to challenge themselves and to earn the grazed knees and stubbed toes that really are necessary to build resilience and confidence. I think a need for adventure resides in all of us.

'So we must encourage children to be part of that wave of enthusiastic amateurs like ourselves. Not necessarily in caves, perhaps.'

Laughter.

'And you might think it strange, having just rescued some kids, that I would like to encourage kids to come underground.'

More laughter.

'But actually, kids do need to be kids, and they need to be allowed to find their own boundaries and to test their own limits. So I plan to spend this year encouraging kids to do just that and to find their inner explorer. Equally importantly to ask parents to let them have a little rope to do that.'

Applause.

'Outdoor activities really do promote physical and mental wellbeing,' I said.

When I was finished, Craig leaned into the microphone. He wanted to focus on Australia, because it had made us who we were. 'I have had the most extraordinary good fortune throughout my life,' he said. 'Probably the single greatest factor is having been born in Australia.'

But Craig's mind, like mine, was on how all of us can be prepared for the next challenges to confront us. 'We must all accept personal responsibility for our destiny. Confronting small everyday challenges and taking responsibility for your actions and their consequences is the only way to be ready for life-defining events.

'There is a temptation to take the easy road ... but we risk never knowing our own strength and what we are capable of. And when we face our test and adversity confronts us, we risk crumbling into a heap and giving up instead of standing up.'

Get out there and do it, we both agreed.

What about the kids?

From the day we left the country, Craig and I wanted to go back and check on the boys. If you help to save someone's life, you want to know how they go on to use it.

How were they doing? Were they suffering nightmares from their time in the cave? Both Craig and I felt a lasting connection to these boys.

In mid-April, nine months after everyone was safely out of the cave, Craig and I were invited back to Thailand as honoured guests of the government. Fiona and Heather came along, as did Millie and Charlie. Our families had earned a nice holiday after all we'd put them through.

We were treated like royalty every step of the way. We had lunch with Don Pramudwinai, the Thai foreign minister. Prime Minister Prayut Chan-o-cha received us along with some of the AFP and Australian Defence Force personnel. It was nice to finally shake the prime minister's hand, having snuck out on him once before. We must have visited a half a dozen temples. We had lights-and-sirens police escorts and even our tuk-tuk ride had a police escort.

At a highly formal ceremony in Bangkok, Craig and I were presented with the Knight Grand Cross (First Class) of the Most Admirable Order of the Direkgunabhorn, a red, gold and silver medal depicting a mythological Garuda bird. The medal was attached to a beautiful green sash with red, white and yellow trim. 'It is worn from the right shoulder to the left hip,' a helpful royal aide leaned over and whispered to us.

That was nice to know, but we had a lot more fun hanging out with Pak at our next stop.

Pak

'We're a long way from Tham Luang cave,' Craig commented as we gazed out the floor-to-ceiling windows of the SO/ Sofitel Bangkok hotel towards Lumpini Park.

That first time we'd met in the cave, Pak said we'd meet up again one day for a drink. I couldn't think of anywhere in the world I'd rather be.

In the nine months since we'd seen each other, he, like us, was now famous in his own country. He had been travelling constantly, giving talks and interviews.

'It's an honour and a big responsibility,' Pak continued. 'But sometimes I also wish my life could just go back to normal. Just be a father and a husband and a doctor and an Army officer.'

We felt much the same.

Pak was everything he had seemed. Warm. Cheerful. Utterly competent and fully in charge. And he was still concerned about the wellbeing of the boys.

'From everything I have heard, they seem to be doing very well,' he said. 'I told you they were good boys.'

Pak's own son was also doing well. 'He missed me when I was away,' Pak said. 'But when I got home, I gave him a giant hug. I couldn't stand the thought that something bad might happen to him.'

I was certain – I know Craig was too – that we would be friends with Pak forever. Across a lifetime, you don't meet many people like him.

Back to the cave

But the boys were the reason we had come back to Thailand, far more than the honours and the thankyous. We flew to Chiang Rai and drove north to Mae Sai.

Things were so much quieter now. The cave was still closed to the public, but it had become a tourist attraction. There were maps and brochures and photos depicting the rescue. Guides were available to tell visitors the story. People were selling things.

On this visit we were accompanied by American expat Josh Morris, who had helped us navigate the Thai generals, and the expat-British caver Vern Unsworth.

Before stepping inside, we stopped to pay our respects at a recently erected statue of Saman Gunan, the ex-Navy SEAL who died in the cave, and at a statue of the Sleeping Lady Nang Non, for whom the mountain range is named.

In a media interview I quipped, 'If we're not out in four hours, come in and help. Bring chocolate and drinks.' That got a nervous laugh.

The cave looked very different without water in it. Some parts were easy to recognise, but other bits, which we knew only by feel, were utterly unfamiliar. In April, we could walk to places that only divers were able to reach in June or July. We hiked and crawled as far as chamber 9, where Coach Ekk and the boys had spent all those days. Then, we walked a few hundred metres past there, to where the assistant coach and his team had tried to find another way out. They left clues. Scratched into the limestone wall with a chunk of rock were two numerals and a letter – 13p – a message that presumably indicated how many people were trapped in the cave. At a nearby spot, someone marked the date – 24 June 2018.

The thirteen

Most of all, we wanted to see Coach Ekk and the boys. We had all been impressed and inspired by them. But Craig and I had some questions for them. What did they remember from the rescue? What did they think of us and the rescue plan? And how were they feeling now that it was all over? We also wanted to clear up some myths that the media had circulated. Did they really drink water dripping from the limestone? Did they really go to the toilet in the cave water? Were they really unable to swim? We had our doubts.

We met Coach Ekk and seven of the boys at the temple. We were touched that so many of them came. The coach and the boys seemed thrilled to welcome us back.

As Craig and I sat cross-legged on the floor, each of the boys knelt before us. Hands together, they bowed, then each of them rested his head for a moment on our knees. Then quickly the boys got up and gave us each a hug. After that, they were lively young people again.

'What do you remember from the day you left the cave?' I asked them.

They all started laughing. 'Good boy, good boy! Jab, jab!'

They thought my soothing pre-anaesthesia blather was hilarious.

They all remembered taking the anti-anxiety tablet and receiving the jabs. They remembered waking up in the field hospital or on the way to the big hospital in Chiang Rai. They remembered nothing in between.

'Ketamine did its job,' Craig said to me.

When I brought up the misconceptions from the media coverage, the answers came back clearly in chorus. Did they drink water that dripped off the rocks? Rubbish, they said. They drank cave water flowing past the bottom of the hill. It was clear until the divers stirred up the silt.

The story of the boys using the cave water for a toilet? Wrong. They dug holes in the dirt across the sump, swimming over with the ever-attentive Navy SEALs each time they had to go.

Were the boys unable to swim? Nonsense, they said. Almost all of them could swim, though none of them had diving experience.

'Our plan to dive you out of the cave while you were sleeping – did that sound sensible? Or did it sound like madness?'

'It was good,' they said.

'Did you think it was dangerous?' Craig asked.

'No, we trusted you.'

That made me shudder. They had no idea how perilous it was. But trapped in the deep, dark, flooded cave with no other way out, what choice did they have?

As Craig and I had travelled around after we left Thailand, we were constantly asked how the boys had coped psychologically. We said they seemed to be doing fine.

We were also asked about the effect on us. 'I was doing two things I love – cave diving and medicine. This was beyond anything we could've imagined, but the outcome was better than we could have hoped for.'

I had a theory about the boys' ability to cope. They were country kids. They grew up in a tough environment. Several of them knew what it meant to be stateless. When you grow up doing hard things, you are ready for the challenges of life when they come.

It was a lesson people everywhere could stand to learn.

ACKNOWLEDGEMENTS

CRAIG AND HARRY

Book writing, like cave diving, is a team sport. Thankfully, we had a world-class team of talented and generous people to help us get our story out in the best possible manner. We are deeply grateful to all of them.

First and always, to our immediate families: Heather, Bruce, Patricia, Ray, Jenny and Bethany. Fiona, James, Charlie, Millie, Amanda and Kristina. Yes, we know how challenging life can be when you care about someone who loves cave diving, but your love, support and forbearance have given us so very much to come home to.

For Craig, fresh adventure is now a fulltime pursuit. Harry still loves his day (and night) jobs caring for patients with Specialist Anaesthetic Services, but he is now spending more time writing, and working on a documentary based on cave science and exploration. He is especially grateful for the wise counsel of Drs James Doube and Andrew Pearce and for the patience of his long-suffering surgical colleagues, all of whom are close friends.

Thanks to the cave-diving community, who have inspired us so often and taught us so much about this passion we share. The Cave Diving Association of Australia, the Cave Diving Group of Great Britain and Northern Ireland, the British Cave Rescue Council and the most ridiculous, high-spirited cave-diving group on earth, the legendary Wet Mules. We are honoured to dive in your midst.

Many dedicated public servants helped us on our way to Thailand: the heroes of the Australian Department of Foreign Affairs and Trade, the Australian Federal Police, the Australian Defence Force, the National Critical Care and Trauma Response Centre, the Australian Embassy staff in Thailand and the Thai Tourist Police, our local liaison and invisible protectors. Without all these people, those boys might never have been rescued from that cave.

By the time we arrived at Tham Luang, Vern Unsworth, Ben Reymenants, Rob Harper, John Volanthen, Rick Stanton and the Thai Navy SEALs had already blazed the trail. Rick and John not only found the children and their coach alive but eloquently conveyed the gravity of the situation to the outside world with the help of Josh Morris. Meanwhile, the Thai and international communities set up crisis support: volunteers poured in from everywhere to provide expertise in meteorology, geology, engineering, catering, communications, media, muscle as well as tonnes of equipment to lower the water and sustain the diving operations. Local climbing and rope-access workers rigged the dry cave section and scoured the bush for alternate entrances. Drilling teams pounded through nearly a kilometre of solid rock. Three brave Thai Navy SEALs, plus the leadership of our new friend for life, Thai Army medic Dr Bhak 'Pak' Loharnshoon, cared for the vulnerable Wild Boars, knowing the adults were in as much danger as the children were. When the sedated kids were ready to be dived out, that perilous journey was led by the four British aces (Rick and John with the addition of Jason Mallinson and Chris Jewell) with special support from three talented young UK divers (Connor, Josh and Jim) and four 'Euro divers' (Erik, Ivan, Claus and Nikko). Working under constant, grinding pressure, these supermen never flinched. When the players and their young coach were delivered to chamber 3, the US pararescue teams, AFP SRG divers, Aussie CD, Chinese divers and Thai Navy and Military medics assessed the kids, then whisked them out of the cave to a field hospital before moving them to the massive hospital in Chiang Rai, where the medical and nursing staffs could ensure their full recovery.

Special personal thanks to Kittanu, Michael, Cameron, Andrew, Jo and Grace of DFAT and the AFP; John Dalla-Zuanna, Peter Wolf and the other directors of the Cave Divers Association of Australia, and Glen McEwen of the AFP. Our heartfelt condolences to the family of the man who tragically died, former Thai Navy SEAL Saman Gunan.

We are fortunate to have such a powerful editorial team in our corner: Co-author Ellis Henican, whose good humour and natural storytelling skills have made these events as heart-pounding to read about as they were to live through. Our tireless researcher Roberta Teer, who knows more about us than we know about ourselves. Transcriber Janis Spidle, who moved raw stories one step closer to literature. And the first-rate publishing team at Penguin Random House Australia, publishers Cate Blake and Nikki Christer, publicist Karen Reid and editor Elena Gomez, as well as copyeditor Elizabeth Cowell, who helped turn all this into a book everyone can be proud of. Juliette Allen, our 'wrangler' who guided us cheerfully and strategically across an unfamiliar media landscape.

One last word about Coach Ekk and the boys: their bravery, their calm and their grace under duress have never ceased to amaze us. Their instant trust in us – a couple of scruffy, middle-aged foreigners who swam up to them one day – is a testament to their openness and decency. It may have saved all our lives. These young people are a credit to their families, their communities and the Kingdom of Thailand.

We wanted to set the story straight and give credit to all those who were involved in this dramatic rescue. While we have become its public face, our role was no more or less important than the roles of hundreds (perhaps thousands) of others. We were fortunate to possess some skills that could contribute to this wonderful outcome. We are endlessly honoured to be in the company of such human greatness.

CAVE RESCUE TIMELINE

2018

23 JUNE – Twelve boys aged between 11 and 16, and their coach, age 25, enter Tham Luang Cave. They were reported missing late afternoon when the park ranger went to close the cave and found bikes at the entrance.

24 JUNE – Vern Unsworth attends and notes that there is water at the T-junction of the cave. A volunteer rescue diver from Chang Rai attempts to dive through the T-junction but is unable to navigate passage.

25 JUNE – The Thai Navy SEALs arrive on site. They dive and walk past the T-junction.

26 JUNE – All rescuers are forced out by flooding. Vern Unsworth writes a note to the Governor and Minister of Interior suggesting three UK cave divers are called to assist. US Indo Pacific Command contacted by Thais and US agree to send 'PJ's' from Okinawa.

27 JUNE – UK divers Rob Harper, Rick Stanton and John Volanthen arrive. Rick and John try to dive the cave. They decide it is too dangerous.

28 JUNE – The flooding worsens. Rick and John make it through to Chamber 3 and rescue the four Thai water workers.

29 JUNE TO 1 JULY – Diving is too hazardous. The search for other entrances and pumping operations begins in earnest. Water diversions begin in the mountains to decrease water influx into the cave system. Rain eases. Drilling sites are identified above the cave. Australian Federal Police arrive on site.

2 JULY – John and Rick enter chamber 9 and find the soccer team. Four Thai Navy SEALs immediately enter the cave, including a doctor and a medic. When they are overdue, three more SEALs are sent in. The SEALs have used too much air to dive the cave and so a total of four end up stuck in the cave instead of just the doctor and medic. The other three manage to escape.

3 TO 5 JULY – Chamber 3 becomes the dive base and is stocked with cylinders and equipment, including body bags. Thai cavers and rope experts begin rigging the 'dry' cave for an extraction. UK divers take MREs into boys and record low oxygen levels in chamber 9.

5 JULY – Harry and Craig agree to assist with rescue, and fly to Chang Rai via Bangkok. An attempt to take a hose to chamber 9 to refresh oxygen levels is commenced.

6 JULY – Harry and Craig arrive. Chris Jewell and Jason Mallinson also arrive at the cave. Suman Gunan drowns between Chambers 3 and 4 while trying to move a bundle of wetsuits to the boys. The attempt to place oxygen hosing into cave is abandoned.

7 JULY – Harry and Craig dive the cave and visit the kids to explain the possible sedation plan. USAF and UK divers test equipment on Thai kids at local swimming pool. USAF lead 'Rehearsal of Concept' (ROC) Drill in carpark to work out logistics of rescue mission. Multiple meetings follow with the Thai leadership and everyone is told a decision will be announced the next morning.

8 JULY – Mission green light. Harry gives anaesthetic 'lecture' to cave divers. DFAT liaison officer Michael Costa tells Harry if a child dies, he and Craig could face legal repercussions. Diplomatic immunity is being sought for the two Australian divers. Rescue Day successful with the first four boys brought out alive.

9 JULY – Rescue day 2 results in four more boys coming out of the cave alive. Weather forecast is worsening and there are major concerns about diving the next and final day.

10 JULY – Rescue day 3 dawns after a night of heavy rain. The divers have major concerns about safety but decide to proceed. The coach then the last four boys come out alive although there are some near misses along the way. As the four Navy Seals reach chamber 3 there is an issue with the water pumps and the area between chambers three and two rapidly begin flooding, and there is a slightly panicked stampede by the remaining rescue teams out of the cave before the exit is sealed by water.

GLOSSARY

air hose A flexible tube that connects the regulator and the demand valve or other equipment that requires compressed air.

booster pump A type of compressor that increases the pressure of gases to very high pressure, usually used for gases other than air (e.g. oxygen).

booties Neoprene foot coverings worn with a wetsuit.

buoyancy compensator A gas-containing bladder that can be adjusted underwater to keep the diver's buoyancy neutral, preventing the diver sinking or floating to the surface uncontrollably.

carabiner (karabiner) A type of coupling with a spring-loaded safety closure used for attaching ropes and other equipment. Used in caving and many other activities.

compressor A machine that increases the pressure of gases. In diving, used for the filling of dive cylinders with air from the atmosphere. Usually powered by petrol or electricity.

cylinder (dive cylinder, tank) A cylindrical vessel that contains high pressure air (or other gases) to be breathed while diving. Usually made of aluminium or steel.

D-rings Fittings on a dive harness that allow for attachment of equipment and accessories.

demand valve A device, usually held in the diver's mouth, which controls the supply of breathing gas by opening when the diver inhales and closing during exhalation. Connected to the regulator by an air hose.

dive harness A webbing harness worn by the diver to which dive cylinders and other diving equipment are attached. May incorporate a buoyancy compensator.

drysuit A type of exposure suit with seals around the neck and wrists that keep the diver completely dry. Usually used in cold water or for very long dives.

duck A short sump or a section with no air space above the water.

eighty-eight An aluminium cylinder of eleven litres volume (traditionally contained eighty-eight cubic feet of air).

exposure suit A garment worn by a diver to protect against cold or injury. May be a wetsuit or a drysuit.

fins Extensions worn on the feet that increase the efficiency of swimming.

flattener A passage in a cave with restricted height. Diving through a flattener usually requires the use of side-mounted cylinders.

full face mask A device that covers the whole face and seals around the head, keeping the diver's face completely dry. Alternative to the half-mask more commonly worn, which covers the eyes and nose only.

guide line Rope or cord laid from the entrance of a cave to the interior, which allows a diver to find their way in the event of not being able to see due to a silt-out or failure of lights.

helmet-mounted lights Underwater electric lights, which are attached to the diver's helmet, rather than being carried in the hand.

LAR rebreather One of a number of types of rebreather manufactured by the German company Dräger.

mouthpiece Rubber or plastic fitting attached to a demand valve, which is easily and comfortably held in the diver's mouth.

MREs (Abbreviation for Meal Ready-to-Eat.) Lightweight packaged field ration used by USA military that does not require refrigeration and is quickly and easily prepared.

QD (Abbreviation for Quick Disconnect.) A fitting to join gas hoses without the use of tools.

rebreather Diving apparatus that allows the diver to breathe the same gas many times over, absorbing the carbon dioxide produced by the diver's body and replacing it with fresh oxygen as required. Much more efficient than SCUBA but at greatly increased complexity and expense.

regulator A device mounted on a dive cylinder that reduces the high pressure of gas inside the cylinder to a lower pressure that is breathable by the diver.

SCUBA (Self Contained Underwater Breathing Apparatus.) A system of equipment including a dive cylinder, regulator and demand valve, which allows a diver to breathe compressed gas underwater.

side-mounted cylinder A technique used in cave diving where the dive cylinders are mounted on the sides of the diver rather than on the diver's back, reducing the diver's profile and allowing the negotiation of low passages underwater.

silt-out A situation where the water becomes filled with fine particles of mud, making it difficult or impossible to see.

sump A section of cave that is filled with water.

switch block A device connected to several air hoses that allows the selection of different sources of gas. For example, it might be used with a full facemask to choose which one of two dive cylinders the diver wishes to breathe from.

wetsuit A type of exposure suit made of neoprene rubber, which allows some water inside the suit. Usually used when the water is not very cold or for shorter dives.

CAVE DIVER'S EQUIPMENT

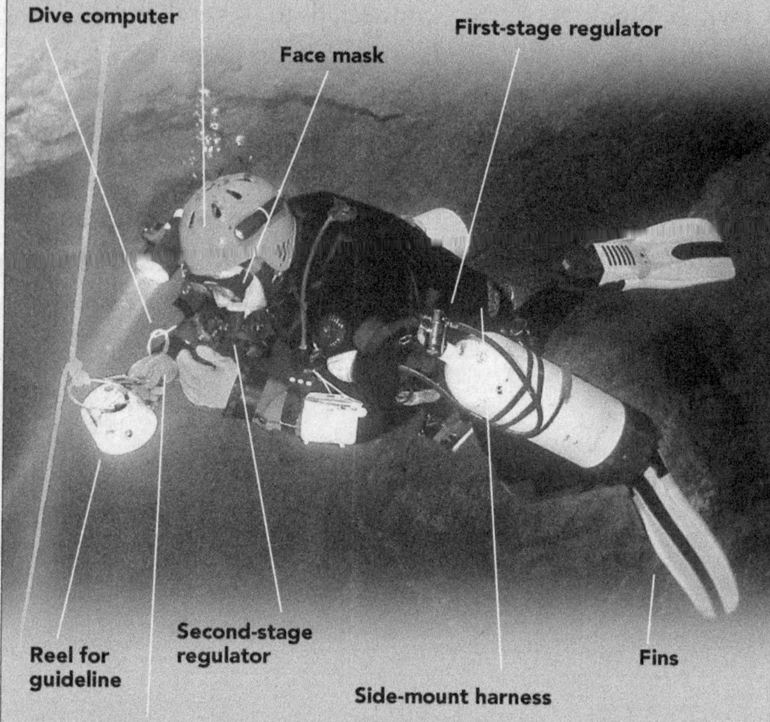

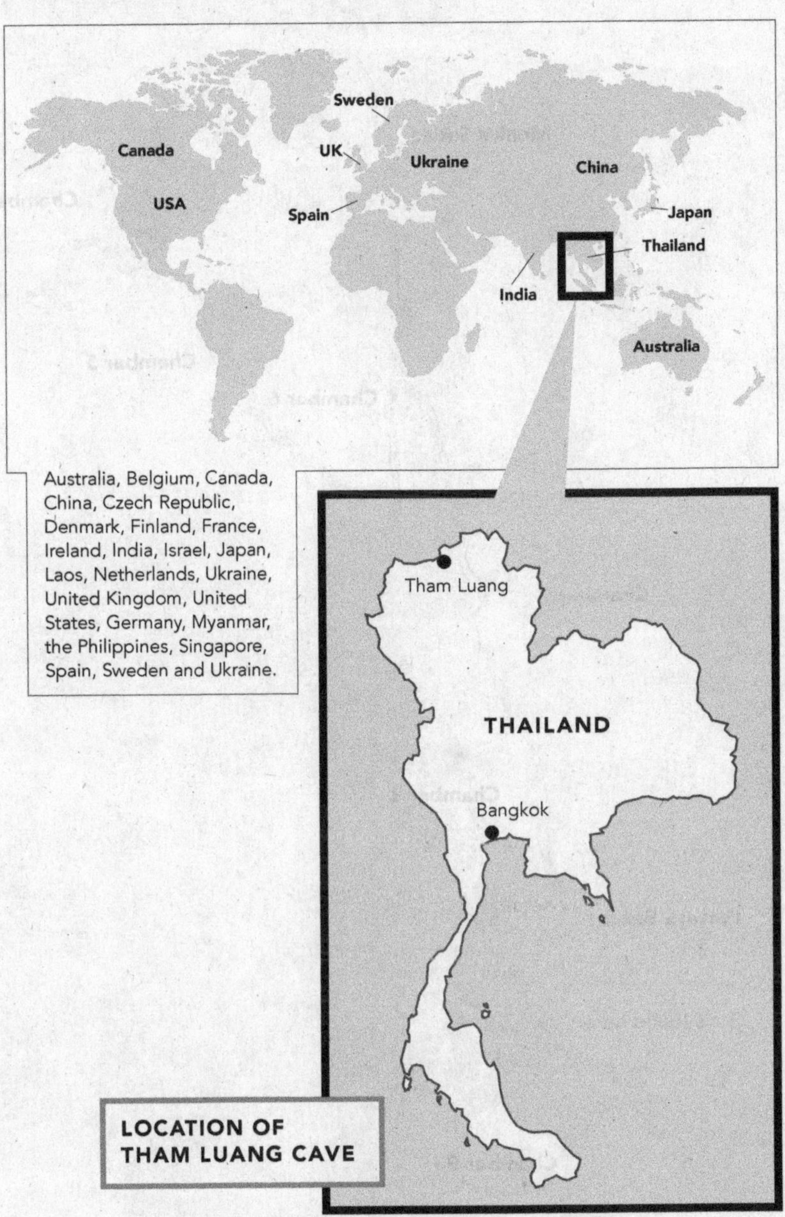
COUNTRIES INVOLVED IN THE INTERNATIONAL RESCUE EFFORT
Sweden
Canada
UK
Ukraine
China
USA
Spain
Japan
Thailand
India
Australia
Australia, Belgium, Canada, China, Czech Republic, Denmark, Finland, France, Ireland, India, Israel, Japan, Laos, Netherlands, Ukraine, United Kingdom, United States, Germany, Myanmar, the Philippines, Singapore, Spain, Sweden and Ukraine.
Tham Luang
THAILAND
Bangkok
LOCATION OF THAM LUANG CAVE

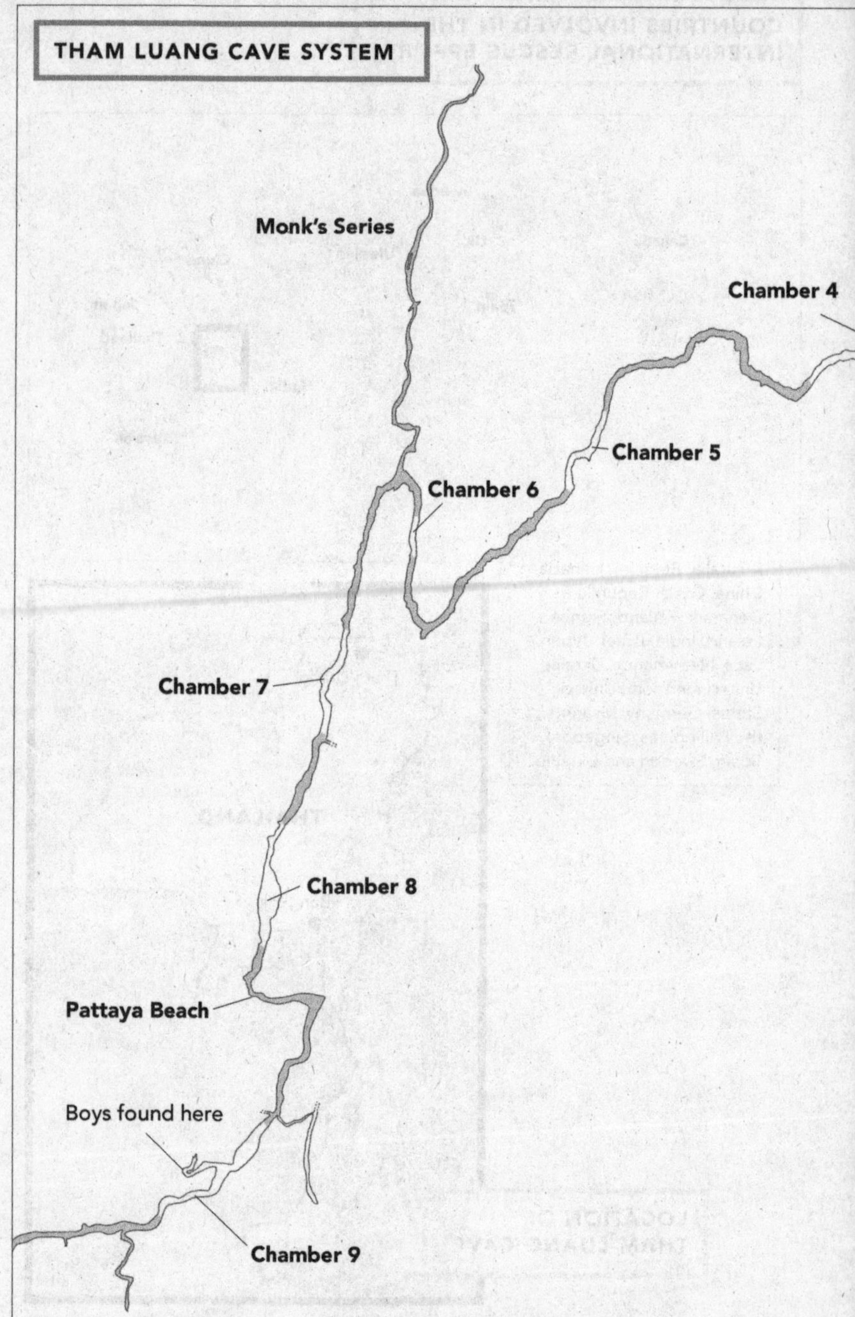
THAM LUANG CAVE SYSTEM
Monk's Series
Chamber 4
Chamber 5
Chamber 6
Chamber 7
Chamber 8
Pattaya Beach
Boys found here
Chamber 9

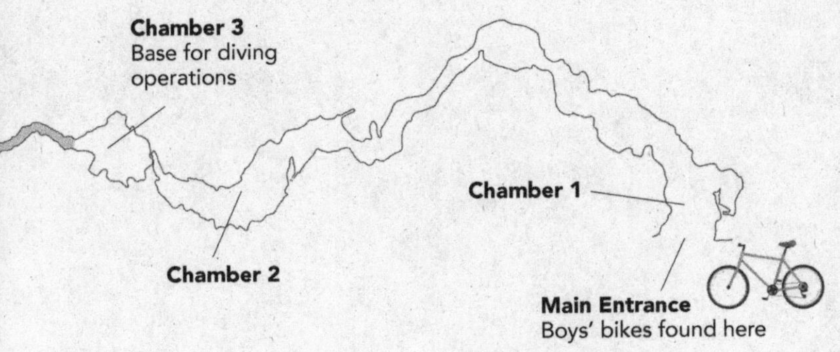

Chamber 3
Base for diving operations
Chamber 1
Chamber 2
Main Entrance
Boys' bikes found here

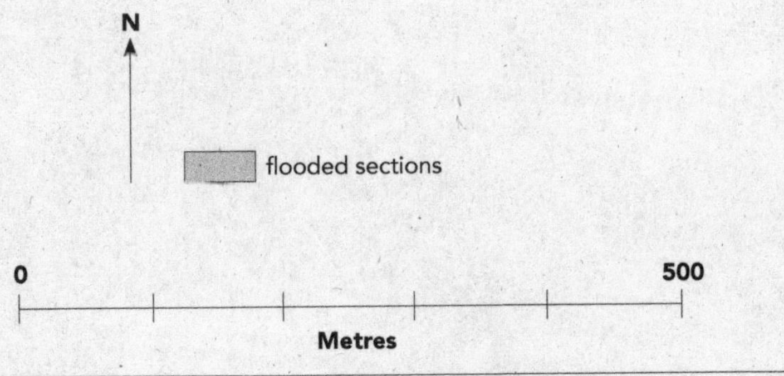

N
flooded sections
0
500
Metres

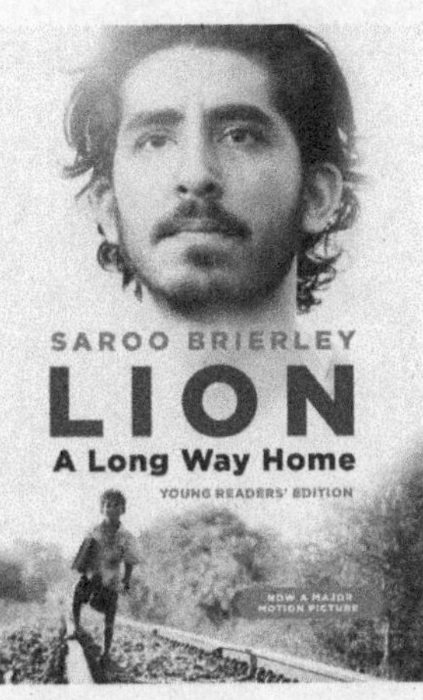

A moving and inspirational true story of survival and triumph against incredible odds. It celebrates the importance of never letting go of what drives the human spirit – hope.

Can you imagine being lost and not finding your way home again?

Saroo Brierley became lost on a train in India at the age of five. Not knowing the name of his family or where he was from, he survived for weeks on the streets of Kolkata, before being taken into an orphanage and adopted by a family in Australia.

Despite being happy in his new home, Saroo always wondered about his origins. He spent hours staring at the map of India on his bedroom wall. He pored over satellite images on Google Earth seeking out landmarks he recognised. And one day, after years of searching, he miraculously found what he was looking for.

Then he set off on a journey back to India to see if he could find his mother.

This inspirational true story of survival and triumph against incredible odds is now a major motion picture starring Dev Patel, David Wenham and Nicole Kidman.

This edition has been specially edited for young readers who want to discover Saroo's extraordinary story for themselves.